Shane Dunphy lives in Wexford, Ireland. He is a writer, musician, sociologist and lecturer. He is the author of several books about his experiences as a child protection worker. He is also a freelance journalist, writing mostly for the *Irish Independent*. Shane is a regular contributor to television and radio, and has produced several documentaries. He teaches Child Development and Social Studies at Waterford College of Further Education.

The Girl from Yesterday

Shane Dunphy

Constable • London

Constable & Robinson Ltd
55–56 Russell Square
London WC1B 4HP
www.constablerobinson.com

First published in the UK by Constable,
an imprint of Constable & Robinson Ltd., 2014

A copy of the British Library Cataloguing in
Publication data is available from the British Library

ISBN 978-1-47210-748-0 (paperback)
ISBN 978-1-47211-124-1 (ebook)

Typeset by TW Typesetting, Plymouth, Devon

Printed and bound in the UK by
CPI Group (UK) Ltd, Croydon, CR0 4YY

1 3 5 7 9 10 8 6 4 2

Remember me when I am gone away,
Gone far away into the silent land;
When you can no more hold me by the hand,
Nor I half turn to go yet turning stay.
Remember me when no more day by day
You tell me of our future that you plann'd;
Only remember me; you understand
It will be late to counsel then or pray.
Yet if you should forget me for a while
And afterwards remember, do not grieve:
For if the darkness and corruption leave
A vestige of the thoughts that once I had,
Better by far you should forget and smile
Than that you should remember and be sad.

Christina Rossetti

'Why d'you come out here?' the girl asked.

'My boss asked me to come,' I answered truthfully.

'Why him want you t' come?'

'I suppose he wants me to get to know you.'

She thought about that one. She was very small for her age, looking more like a five- or six-year-old than her ten years. We sat in the unkempt grass of the field behind her family's house. Her long hair was all curls and the same colour as corn.

'Why he want that?'

'I don't know. Do you mind my hanging out with you and your brothers and sisters?'

She made an expansive shrug.

'I don' mind.'

I watched swifts chasing insects across the sky like fighter planes. We could hear the sea less than a hundred yards away.

'I like bashin',' the girl said, as if this was a profound statement.

'Bashing?'

'Yeah. Want to help me bash?'

I couldn't think of a reason not to.

'Do you have a spare basher?'

She giggled, a delightful, musical sound.

'I don't gots no basher,' she said. 'I uses a stick. Le's get you a stick. You'll need a big one.'

1

She pushed herself up off the ground and skipped off.

We found a sturdy hazel rod in a clutch of trees that formed a border between two fields.

'So . . . how do we bash?' I asked.

'I will show you,' she said, and taking my hand led me to a small field, barely more than a copse, that had grass, cow parsley and ragwort that had grown taller than she was. 'Now, we gots to bash a passageway through all these here weeds, and make a hideout in the middle.'

Bashing. Now I understood.

For a tiny thing, she had an impressive bashing arm. She used a thin ash branch, but she whipped it with such force she carved her way through the undergrowth at a tremendous pace. Every now and then she would pass a comment on my work or bark an instruction:

'Tha's some good bashin' there, mister,' or 'Not too much on tha' side – we wants the passage to be small, okay?'

In about forty-five minutes we had carved our way right into the centre of the field, and the girl, perhaps a little tired now, supervised my creating a circular space, like small room. She was remarkably thorough, even taking up the cut pieces of vegetation and throwing them away, so we were left with a patch of grass with a few stumps poking through, but mostly flat.

'There you go,' I said. 'All done. So what are you going to do now? Plant some flowers here? Dig some holes?'

'I'm gonna cover up the doorway,' she said solemnly.

'That door we made to get in? Out at the start of the field?'

'Yes.'

'Why?'

' 'Cause this is a secret hiding place.'

I nodded conspiratorially.

'For when you're playing hide and seek?'

'No,' she said. 'For when I need to hide.'

PROLOGUE

It did not rain on the day we buried Lonnie Whitmore – the sky stayed a dull metallic grey, but it did not open and soak the small congregation. A murder of crows perched atop a half-dead ash tree, just off the path that ran past the freshly excavated grave. I thought this fitting, but the black-feathered birds did not take to the sky in a flurry of ominous beating wings as the coffin was lowered.

The ceremony was . . . nice.

I stood apart from the group and wondered what I was going to do. The priest droned his way through a decade of the rosary. Three of the thirty or so people gathered responded in the appropriate places. The rest looked numb and ill at ease.

Lonnie had been my friend. Maybe even my best friend. He had died suddenly a week previously of a heart attack caused by a congenital problem associated with his particular form of dwarfism. Lonnie had spent most of his life locked away from prying eyes by a family who were ashamed of how he looked. When he finally came out of hiding he blossomed: I knew him as a proud, funny, irreverent man who apologized to nobody for his apparent strangeness. When he died he was manager of a crèche for children with special needs and in a relationship with Tush Cogley, a pretty colleague. He left the world a happy, fulfilled man.

I had not seen Lonnie at all the month before he died. We hadn't fallen out nor were we estranged in any real sense: life just seemed to get in the way. I had taken on more responsibility in Drumlin Therapeutic Training Unit, a day care centre for adults with intellectual disabilities where I worked, and he had taken over the running of the crèche we had both wrestled from the brink of closure, bringing it to even greater levels of excellence.

I told myself that he had a girlfriend, his career was taking off and that he did not need me hanging around, getting in the way. But the truth was I had been remiss: a bad, neglectful friend. I realized too late that Lonnie's first faltering steps as a manager would have been a time he really needed a listening ear; at the time I hadn't wanted to know, burying myself in my own work. On the day I was told of Lonnie's passing, I checked my phone and saw that I had three messages from him going back over a fortnight, all suggesting we get together and catch up. I had not responded to any of them.

I watched as my boss, Tristan Fowler, and some of my fellow workers from Drumlin huddled by a grove of ash, chatting quietly, solemnly.

'I'll see you around, Lonnie,' I said under my breath, and as the world misted in tears I walked through the cracked and lopsided gravestones to the road.

Cowardice had become my modus operandi. I scrawled a letter of resignation sitting at the little kitchen table of my rented cottage. My plan was to drop it through Drumlin's letterbox on my way out of town. I put a month's rent in an envelope and added a note of apology to Barney, my aged but surprisingly sprightly landlord, informing him cryptically that my circumstances had changed, and thanking him for all his help and support during the three years of my tenancy. It took me all of an hour to pack up what I needed, and I boxed the rest and left what was still usable outside the local community centre, a stuttering message on the parish priest's voicemail asking him to pass my garden tools and odds and ends on to someone who might need them – I had no room for such luxuries, and did not see myself having much call for them in the immediate future.

Tush answered the door to me on my third ring. She was in her late twenties, a good ten years younger than me, and her pretty face was stained red from crying, her blonde hair tousled and uncharacteristically awry. She said nothing but stepped aside to allow me into the little house on the mountainside she and Lonnie had shared.

'D'you want tea?' she asked. 'I was just about to make something.'

'No, thank you,' I said. 'I'm not staying long. I just . . . I just wanted to see how you are.'

'I'm shit, thank you very much,' she said, sitting on the couch and motioning at a chair opposite. I perched on it awkwardly. I shouldn't have come. I could have made a clean getaway.

'Yeah,' I said, looking at my hands and then the floor. 'I bet you are.'

'I don't know what to do with myself,' she said. 'I clean the place and wash clothes and pick flowers for the window, just like we used to do – I mean, you know the state he kept this place in before I moved here . . .'

I nodded and tried to smile. When Tristan and I first visited Lonnie, the house had sagged under the weight of neglect, every room a clutter of oddments, religious paraphernalia, old newspapers and dust. When Tush arrived she had immediately brought a woman's touch without purging the place of Lonnie's larger-than-life personality: if anything she had allowed his tastes to take shape in a more controlled, less frenetic way. A plastic figurine of Jesus stood on the mantelpiece beside an action figure of Darth Vader, the two leaning in to one another as if they were confiding secrets. On the wall above was a framed poster of Lonnie's beloved Sex Pistols, John Lydon snarling at the camera as if he was offended by it.

'This is your home, Tush,' I said. 'That hasn't changed.'

'I don't know if I can continue living here without him.'

'You can always sell the place,' I said, 'not that you'd get much for it right now.'

She said nothing to that, instead blowing her nose loudly into a tissue.

'What do you want, Shane?'

'To see that you were okay, and to say goodbye.'

She looked up sharply.

'Where are you going?'

'I don't know. Away from here. Somewhere new.'

'But your job. Your house. Millie . . .'

'Millie is coming with me, of course,' I said, referring to the greyhound Lonnie and I had more or less shared before we started to drift. 'I've resigned from my job, and I've given back the keys to the cottage.'

'Why?'

'I came here three years ago to start a new life, a different life, and I ended up getting sucked right back into the same patterns of behaviour, a similar type of job; I might as well have stayed in the city. Lonnie dying has made me realize that I have nothing to tie me here.'

'What about me?' she said, hurt dripping from her voice. 'What about all your friends and all the clients at Drumlin and . . . and the *life* you've built here? Have you given it any thought at all?'

'I've been thinking about it a lot, Tush. For a long while, now. Since I left Lonnie to run Little Scamps, if I'm honest.'

She stood up and walked to the window.

'Lonnie really looked up to you,' she said. 'You were some kind of hero to him: he really aspired to be like you.'

'He never had any fucking sense,' I said, fighting hard not to start bawling.

'He thought you had it all sussed,' Tush continued as if I hadn't spoken. 'Oh, he'd make jokes about you, call you a bleeding-heart hippy and so on, but it was all to hide his complete idolatry of you. You saved him, you see. And despite everything, you always treated him like a person, not a walking condition.'

'Not always,' I said quietly.

'He was planning to go back to college and get his degree,' Tush said. "I'll have letters after my name like the beardy fella", he'd say. He was going to go at night. He laughed that you might even end up teaching him – you still do some part-time teaching, don't you? He would have liked that, I think. He'd have been so proud.'

'That would have been nice. A bit odd, but nice.'

'He thought you had all the answers. But you don't at all, do you?'

'No,' I said.

'You're just as messed up and scared as any of the rest of us.'

There didn't seem to be anything to say to that. I sat and looked at her as she gazed at some spot on the horizon.

'Go on,' she said after a time, 'run away. You won't find peace or whatever it is you're looking for anywhere else, you know. Guess what? You'll bring whatever crap you've got floating in that black cloud you carry around over your head with you to whereever you're going.'

I stood up. She watched me, her eyes wet, her face accusing.

'You're a coward,' she said, no anger in her voice now, just pain.

'I know. I never pretended to be anything else.'

'Yes you did. You let us think you knew it all.'

'If that's true, I'm sorry.'

I began to back towards the door in an undignified shuffle.

'Not as sorry as I am,' Tush said, and then I was at the door, then outside in the cool air. I started the engine of the Austin and did not look back.

I had no plan, had not really thought about where I might go. I let the road lead me, and simply drove. When I got tired, I stopped and took Millie for a walk along the hard shoulder for a bit. When I got hungry I had something to eat, but mainly I travelled, watching as the landscape got more rugged and more grey the further west I went.

My first night on the road I got a room in a small B & B that didn't mind dogs, and rose the following morning before seven and slipped away. It was pleasant enough weather, in the middle of August: not quite blazing sunshine, but it was reasonably dry and I made good speed, arriving into the small town of Garshaigh around lunch time on my second day. I pulled up outside the only hotel, a place called The Grapevine, and sat back, stretching my shoulders. Millie was splayed out in the back seat, having somehow contorted herself into a position that did not look even remotely comfortable. I often marvelled at how her spine seemed to be able to twist effortlessly into any convolution. I clicked my tongue and she opened one eye, surveying me ruefully.

'Let's see what this place has to offer,' I suggested.

The dog sighed with a tone of unveiled contempt and rolled over, showing her back to me, her paws tucked under her now.

'Suit yourself,' I said, and got out, leaving the greyhound to her slumbers.

Garshaigh was an average Irish country town. It took me ten minutes to walk the main street from end to end (I knew I had left the burgh when I found myself back out in the countryside again), and I counted six pubs, a post office, a tiny chemist that seemed to cater for the needs of humans and animals alike, myriad clothes shops, many of which looked as if they had been warped into the present from the 1950s, a reasonably sized supermarket, a decent-looking café, a small newsagent and a second-hand bookshop that looked like it could keep me occupied for a while.

A brief perusal of a notice board erected for the few tourists who may stop on their way to somewhere else informed me that Garshaigh was one of the most westerly towns in Ireland, an old Norman stronghold that had once been of tactical significance because of its proximity to the coast.

One of the most westerly towns in Ireland. I read the line again. I couldn't really flee any further. I had basically run out of land. The idea pleased me in a twisted kind of way.

I strolled back to the hotel and booked a room, informing the middle-aged woman behind the reception desk that Millie would be joining me.

'We don't usually permit dogs, sir.'

'Usually?' I raised an eyebrow.

'We might be encouraged to make an exception.'

I nodded, casting a quick eye about me – the place looked as if it hadn't been redecorated in about thirty years, and I had a suspicion that I might be the only guest. But I smiled in as charming a way as I could muster.

'I see. Would there be a particular sum of money that might induce such an exception to be made, d'you think?'

'Why don't you suggest an amount, and we'll work from there?'

Thirty euro per night ended up settling the matter, which hit my pocket pretty hard, but wasn't as much as I had expected. I went back out to the car and physically hefted Millie out onto the pavement. She made a great show of stretching and yawning, letting me know in no uncertain terms that she was not happy about her change in situation, but I tried to ignore her accusatory glances. I was fiddling about in the boot when I heard a trundling sound, and, looking up, saw a chubby, blond-haired man in a wheelchair stopping beside me.

'D'you need a hand with your bags?' he asked. 'You can just rest one across the arms of the chair and I'll bring it in for you.'

'Thanks, but I didn't bring much,' I said.

'I'm Jeff,' he said. 'Jeff McKinney. I work in the hotel. Live here too, so I'm always around if you need me.'

'Well, I'll holler if anything comes up,' I said, 'but right now I can just about manage on my own.'

He hung about as if I might say something else or perhaps offer him a tip for the services I didn't require. When neither of these things was forthcoming, he rolled off in a disgruntled kind of way.

I turned my attention back to the boot's contents. I was beginning to get a sense of how rushed and ill-conceived my flight had been. Right at the back were my precious musical instruments. In front of them were some cardboard boxes into which I had packed my CDs, vinyl, some fairly ancient (and at this stage barely playable) audio tapes, as well as most of my books and some favourite pictures and knick-knacks. I had managed to get my stereo in there as well, and that just about left room for a modest suitcase for a random selection of my clothes. Everything else I had jettisoned.

'I don't know if you'd call it travelling light,' I muttered in the direction of my dog who had buried her nose in a flower bed and paid me absolutely no heed, 'but we'd better not get invited to any black tie events.'

The room was actually quite nice, and when I had put what few items of clothing I had brought away in the wardrobe I sprawled on the bed, with Millie deigning to sit beside me. The TV only seemed to show one grainy station, so having no other option I watched Angela Lansbury solve a murder that took place during an amateur production of the musical *Oklahoma* – the culprit turned out to be the unpleasant second wife of an old friend of Angela's – the motive seemed unclear to me, but it appeared that money was involved somewhere. Dick Van Dyke followed, solving a murder in the hospital where he worked. The culprit turned out to be the unpleasant and much younger third wife of the now deceased patient, and this time I could see quite clearly that the motive was money. Feeling smug that I had followed the clues just as well as Van Dyke's Doctor Sloan, I discovered that the next item on the schedule was Andy Griffith in *Matlock*. I wasn't sure if I could stomach any more elderly crime fighters, so decided to head out and get a late lunch.

Millie followed dolefully on her lead (she was clearly a closet *Matlock* fan) as I walked the short distance to the café I had spotted earlier. She occasionally stopped to sniff something smeared onto the pavement or to look pointedly at another dog. I paused in my leisurely amble to allow her to acclimatize herself to her surroundings.

The café was pretty, bedecked with flowers and red-check tablecloths, and warm with the smell of freshly baked bread and just-made coffee. The waitress was about my age and pretty in a natural, easy kind of way and, as she scratched Millie behind the ears, she said that she didn't mind such a well-behaved dog sitting under the table at all. Millie threw me a scorn-filled look: *See? She thinks I'm well behaved!* And slunk over to curl about my feet. I ordered a ham and cheese sandwich (my repast of choice in a new place – it is as simple an item as you could imagine, but I am constantly amazed at the ways people find to make a botch of it) with English mustard on the side and a mug of black coffee. When the food arrived, it was just as I had ordered, and the java was as good as its aroma promised. I decided to hang out for an hour or so.

Later I followed the narrow road that wound down to the coast, a five-mile walk that terminated in a good mile and a half over loose sand and dunes that sloped downhill to a wild, deserted beach. Millie took off as soon as I removed her lead and plunged into the breakers, emerging dripping and shivering. I stood and looked out at the heaving waves for a few moments, realizing for the first time in what seemed like forever that my mind was empty and that I felt absolutely nothing. I walked to the waterline and shed my clothes, caring not one bit if anyone was around, and plunged into the icy water, feeling the first surging wave knock every last ounce of breath from my body. With gritted teeth I forced myself forward until I felt my feet lifting from the sandy floor, and then struck out for the horizon. I swam ferociously for about ten minutes, then stopped and looked back at the shoreline. I was surprised at how far I had gone from the beach. Millie was standing at the water's edge, her ears standing right up, her tail between her legs. I hung there, suspended in the brine for a few moments, then put my arms by my side, pointed my toes downward and allowed myself to sink. Down I went, down, feeling the ocean boom and roar about me. Space and void opened up on every side. Colours of blue, green and azure shimmered dreamily. As I continued to drift downwards I felt a deep sense of contentment, of belonging.

You could stay here, a voice seemed to say from the depths below. *There's no pain, no fear, no anger.*

I was no longer cold, the effort of driving myself through the crashing whiteheads had warmed my muscles, and down in the deep blue, I felt calm, easy.

Then another voice resonated about me.

You let us think you knew it all. That you had all the answers.

Tush's words echoed in the murk, accusing, filled with hurt and regret. I covered my ears but the voice was coming from inside me, too, and in a great motion I kicked and shot towards the distant surface, a trail of bubbles streaming behind me. It seemed like hours before I broke into the air with a roar. Under the impassive sky I lay on my back, gulping oxygen in sobbing gasps. Through the sound of the sea and my own crying I heard Millie barking, calling me back.

I bought a bag of dry dog food and bottle of Bushmills Irish whiskey in the grocer's and took them up to the room. As my canine friend enjoyed her evening meal I switched on the electric kettle the hotel thoughtfully provided and made myself a hot toddy. On TV, Father Dowling, as played by Tom Bosley, was investigating the murder of a charity fundraiser. I strongly suspected that his much younger wife might be behind it, but didn't want to tell the meddling priest how to do his job.

'D'you think Sister Steve is good-looking?' I asked Millie.

She didn't seem to really care. I took a sip of my drink. It tasted like another sip might be needed, and soon.

'Well, I do,' I said. 'Here's to you, Sister.'

Tracy Nelson, who played Sister Steve on the show, didn't seem all that interested in my opinion of her attractiveness, but the night was young and I had absolutely nothing else to do.

Two more hot Bushmills brought me through Father Dowling, which, to my delight (the drunker I got, the lower my standards as regards entertainment went), was followed by an episode of *Columbo* in which William Shatner, a particular favourite of mine, starred as a radio talk-show host accused of killing a colleague. Shatner seemed to have it all pretty well sewn up, but I had a suspicion that the rumpled Peter Falk might just find a way through the carefully laid trail of clues and minor mistakes that seemed to be suggesting that the former Captain Kirk might not be as innocent as he claimed.

By the time Columbo sprang his trap, I was so drunk I had stopped following what was going on at all. Millie was snoring gently, head resting on my leg. I must have dozed off because suddenly I realized that the room was dark and an episode of *Quincy* was now running on the television. I fumbled around for the remote control to turn the set off, but couldn't seem to find it. I struggled to get up to look for it, but somehow only managed to end up sitting on the floor. I stayed there for a bit, looking about me in a befuddled way.

'Jesus, look at the state of you,' a voice said.

I squinted stupidly and followed the sound of the voice, trying once again to get up, still unsuccessfully.

'I think you may give that up as a bad job,' the voice spoke again, and this time I saw Lonnie Whitmore perched on the room's only chair – squatting on his haunches on the arm of the chair as he had a habit of doing.

'Hey Lonnie,' I slurred. 'I wasn't expecting you.'

'Aw, we were never ones to stand on ceremony,' Lonnie smiled.

He was wearing a pair of deep orange dungarees with

peppermint blue, diamante-encrusted Converse high tops and a shirt so purple it hurt my teeth.

'What're you doin' here, Lonnie?' I asked, struggling to form sentences.

'I came to check up on Millie,' my dead friend said. 'I wasn't sure you'd be in a fit state to look after her.'

'Whaddaya mean?' I said, a little more sharply, 'I always look after her right properly.'

'You came close to abandoning her on the beach today.'

I lowered my eyes at that.

'I on'y went for swim.'

'Where were you swimming to, you pathetic git,' Lonnie barked back, 'fucking America?'

I cast about for the bottle and found it on the edge of the bed.

'Want a drink?'

Lonnie shrugged and was suddenly sitting beside me. I hadn't seen him moving, but then it was turning into that sort of night. I poured myself a glug, and then realized that I didn't have another glass.

'You'll have to use th' bottle,' I said, passing it to him.

'I'm surprised you're bothering with the facade of a glass,' Lonnie muttered, taking a swig.

'My mammy brung me up right,' I retorted.

We drank in silence. Millie stirred, but settled again instantaneously.

'What're you going to do, Shane?'

'Get more drunker.'

'I mean tomorrow. And the day after that.'

I sighed deeply and looked at him from the corner of my eye. He didn't look like a ghost. Do ghosts drink whiskey? Do they wear severely clashing, day-glo-coloured clothes?

'You are fucking demised, Lonnie,' I said accusingly. 'You had a goddam heart attack.'

'Death is relative,' Lonnie said sagely.

'What the hell does that mean?' I asked.

'I have no idea,' Lonnie said, and we both burst out laughing.

'I'm gonna stay in this place for a while, I think,' I said.

'It's kind of a shit hole,' Lonnie said.

'I don't know where else to go,' I said.

'Why don't you go home?' Lonnie asked, putting his big hand on my shoulder. 'Go home to Tush and to Tristan and to all the people who care about you.'

'Can't,' I said, shaking my head, tears streaming down my face.

'Why not?'

'I fucked up, Lonnie,' I said. 'I fucked up real bad, and I . . . I need to jus' get 'way from ev'rybody. 'Kay?'

My friend squeezed my arm and nodded sadly.

'All right then. You know best, I suppose.'

I laughed bitterly.

'I don' know anythin'. That's the fuckin' problem.'

I took a deep gulp from my glass, feeling the liquor burn its way down my throat.

'I think maybe you ought to lay off the hard stuff for a bit, don't you?' Lonnie said. 'You're going to be awfully sick in the morning.'

I blinked, looking at my empty glass and the three-quarter-empty bottle. Lonnie had only had a few sips from it. And Millie hadn't had any at all.

'I'm tired, man,' I said. 'Think I need t' sleep a bit.'

Lonnie hopped up and got his hands under my armpits, hoisting me back up onto the bed – he was comparably as strong as an ant – I was always amazed by it.

'You go on and sleep,' Lonnie said, pulling the duvet over me.

'Yeah,' I said, already drifting. 'You gonna stay?'

'I'll be around,' Lonnie said. 'Don't you worry about it.'

'I'm glad,' I said, the words all mashing together. 'I'm glad you're a zombie 'r a vampire 'r somethin'. Be nice havin' you about again.'

Then I was gone.

I had a ferocious hangover in the morning, but despite my throbbing head and heaving guts Millie needed to be let out for her morning ablutions. After she had taken what seemed like an age to find just the right place to relieve herself, I got some bottled water from the bar of the hotel (which never seemed to close), tried to drink some and then went back to bed for four hours. When I woke again, I still felt like hell but I was more or less able to function, and after a shower and change of clothes children didn't run screaming when I walked past.

As I left the hotel, Jeff McKinney, who was sitting in the lobby looking bored, hailed me.

'You have a visitor last night?'

I froze.

'Why do you ask that?'

'Thought I heard voices coming from your room.'

'Jeff, why were you listening to any noises coming from my room?'

He blustered a bit at that.

'I just had to do something for one of the other guests at that end of the house . . .'

'Are there any other guests?'

He made an excuse and disappeared down the corridor to the dining room.

I went out to the Austin, Millie trailing after me, sat inside the car and switched on the radio to catch the early afternoon news. Ireland hadn't snapped out of the economic recession

17

overnight, it seemed, and unemployment, crime and general misery were widespread. So nothing much had changed.

We had lunch in the little café again, and I felt some life returning as the caffeine did its work. I had a vague memory of talking to Lonnie the previous night, but that was something I did not want to spend too much time pondering – I had seen some strange things over the years, and while I applied a healthy pinch of salt to most of it, I tried to keep in mind that I had spent a good deal of my life working with people *in extremis*, and that meant that, sometimes quite literally, anything could happen. My recollection of the visitation was that it had been comforting and supportive, at any rate, so I figured the best thing to do might be simply to write it off as a little wish fulfilment and move on – I was reasonably certain that a degree of unresolved grief, combined with a liberal dousing of Irish whiskey, was the main culprit.

As I sipped my third cup of coffee, I watched people come and go outside the window. Garshaigh was a bustling little town. Everywhere I looked I saw industry and autonomy. It made me feel slightly guilty. I really did have to work out some sort of plan of action for what I was going to do with my life for the immediate future. Without beating around the bush, I needed money: I had some savings which I was living off, but they would not last forever, and staying in the hotel was going to eat a huge hole in my resources before very long. I was, on a temporary basis at the very least, in need of a job.

But what kind of job? And in this age of swollen dole queues and emaciated bank statements would there even be any gainful employment to be had?

I knew for certain that I did not want to do anything even resembling social care work – I had washed my hands of it twice before, and had always ended up being drawn back in. I had always blamed everyone else for this: people laying their problems at my feet or circumstances conspiring to place me in close proximity to children in need of help, but I now realized that it was my responses to events and to the people I found myself in contact with that had brought me back into the caring professions and child protection. I was determined that was not going to happen again: the work hurt me too much and caused me to do things, make decisions, I hated. I realized that I did not like that version of 'me', 'Shane the child protection worker', one little bit. He was judgemental, self-serving and could be quite a bully at times. People around him got hurt. I wanted to leave him behind and find out who I really was when I was away from all that drama and anguish.

I had tried my hand at living off my music when I moved to the Midlands three years ago, and had been quite successful, but playing music in local pubs had brought me in contact with the individuals who had eventually led me to Drumlin Therapeutic Training Unit, where I had met Lonnie, so I summarily dismissed being a musician as a course of action.

I was running out of options. Looking over my meagre skill set, I was left with teaching, which I had done on a part-time basis for some years to supplement my income, and writing, which was something I occasionally flirted with in terms of the odd article for a local newspaper or, from time to time, for the nationals. I had done one or two academic articles too, some of which had been quite well received. Writing didn't pay much (sometimes it had paid me nothing at all) but I enjoyed it, and I reasoned that it probably wouldn't put me in too great a risk of coming in contact with any child protection situations.

That said, a teaching gig seemed the most likely option. From the foot traffic on the street outside I judged that there had to be a good-sized school in the town, and that probably meant night classes. It being August, I reasoned they might be looking for new teaching staff. I thought that would be a sensible first port of call.

After one more cup of coffee.

The pretty waitress (whose name was Carla) told me how to find the school. It was an ancient-looking grey stone structure, all flat roofs and metal-framed windows, with a tangible air of emptiness about it a fortnight before the students were to return. The school administrator, a bombastic, heavily built woman with violently red hair, told me to wait on a plastic chair just inside the heavy wooden front door, and after what felt like an age but was more like ten minutes a harangued-looking man in his late fifties wearing a muted grey suit, which matched his grey hair and grey skin perfectly, came out and snapped his hand in my direction.

'George Taylor,' he said. 'I'm principal of St Smoling's, and that makes me head of the night school also.'

'Shane Dunphy,' I said, getting up and shaking his hand, which was what I assumed he wanted me to do with it.

'Can we talk as we walk, Mr Dunphy, I have a hundred and one things to do today and we are severely understaffed. The school used to have two caretakers and a porter. Under the current economic restrictions we have one caretaker, despite the fact that the number of students has almost doubled. Do you know what that means?'

'Um . . .' It felt like I was being given a test which I had not studied for.

'It means that I now have maintenance tasks to do on top of my usual workload,' George Taylor strode briskly away from me. I gave chase.

'We have five gaps on our night-class timetable,' the principal said as he led me out the back of the building to what looked like an ancient tool shed. 'Childcare, conversational

French, Chinese cooking, motorcycle maintenance and tropical fish keeping.'

'A mixed bag,' I said.

George Taylor removed his jacket and hung it on a polished wooden hanger which he then returned to a hook on the door of the shed. He tucked his grey silk tie inside his shirt in a deft movement.

'Do you have qualifications or experience in any of those subjects, Mr Dunphy?'

'Yes. I have both in the area of childcare.'

'Excellent. And you can furnish me with references from your professional and teaching experience?'

I took an envelope from my shoulder bag and held it out to him.

'My CV, complete with written references and the contact details of previous employers who will vouch for me.'

George Taylor went into the shed and came out a second later carrying a large blade strimmer in one hand and a pair of plastic goggles in the other.

'You may leave it with Regina in the front office. If all is as you say, you can consider the job yours. You will teach for three hours, two evenings a week. If you've done this kind of work before you will know what to expect.'

I nodded. 'That's it then?'

George Taylor pulled a ripcord on the strimmer and the machine roared into life.

'I'll call you with start-up details and a list of your students. The classes are already quite full,' he shouted over the engine. 'Now, I have work to do. Would you mind showing yourself out?'

The offices of the *Western News* filled two rooms over the supermarket. The editor was a thin, owl-like man in his forties called Robert Chaplin. He smelt of cigarettes and cheap after-shave. An out-of-date computer hummed on his desk, which was otherwise buried in scraps of paper, fast-food wrappers and stained coffee mugs.

'What makes you think we need any more staff?' Chaplin said tersely. 'We haven't fucking advertised.'

'I'm just calling in on spec,' I said. 'I've never gotten a job yet that I applied for through a want ad. I've done some writing in the past, thought I might see if you were looking to fill some column inches.'

'Who'd you write for?'

I told him. He raised an eyebrow.

'Jim Davitt still writing for the *Citizen*?'

'He edited me a couple of times.'

'So you did all this as a freelancer?'

I told him I did.

'Ever had a more full-time writing gig?'

'Nope. There have been some times when I was writing a few thousand words a week, but I was never full time in the office, no.'

'I mean, it's totally different when you're doing it all day every day. How do I know you won't dry up on me?'

'I've never missed a deadline. Never come up short on an assignment.'

Chaplin nodded.

'And your background is all this child abuse stuff? You're what . . . a social worker or something?'

'Something. To be honest, I'm looking for a change of scene, a change of job. Start me on the bottom rung of the ladder and see what I can do. If you don't like what I produce, cut me loose. You'll have lost nothing.'

The thin man coughed and looked at the CV I had given him. He pulled the keyboard of his computer towards him and tapped loudly on it, making a sound like a machine gun. He waited for a moment then clicked the mouse. He turned the screen a little to accommodate glare, then pondered the display. I knew he was looking up one of the pieces I had written, and waited for his verdict.

'Okay, you can write,' he said at last. 'But you're a bit fucking wordy, and you tend to put yourself into everything. My readers aren't interested in you or your deepest darkest feelings. I run a local rag that lets Granny McDuff know when the flower show is on and who has been up in court for stealing knickers off their neighbour's washing line. That's what my audience want to read, and they don't give a flying fuck what you think about any of it.'

'I realize that, but thank you for flagging it up,' I said.

'You're very welcome.'

'So?'

'So what?'

'So would you like to try me out?'

Chaplin sighed.

'I don't fucking know. Look, I'll tell you what. Do you have a car?'

'I do.'

'Go along to this,' he rooted around until he found a flyer, which he passed over to me. It advertised a gathering to protest the re-zoning of some bogland. I saw from the date that it was happening that evening at eight. 'Write me eight hundred words on what happens. Then we'll talk again.'

'Right you be.'

I stood.

'I'll hang on to your CV,' he said, turning back to the monitor. 'I might give it a bit of a lookover again at some stage when I have a free moment.'

'All right then,' I said. 'I'll give you a shout tomorrow.'

23

'I'll be here.'

The protest meeting proved to be mind-numbingly boring, but I managed to put together an article that made the local people look like courageous campaigners, the very soul of the land at stake as soulless foreign developers tried to steam roll over vital swathes of ecosystem. Which was, in fairness, true.

Chaplin read it thoughtfully.

'This is good,' he said when he was done. 'And very clean. You can punctuate and you know how to use a spell check. And I believe this is eight hundred words bang on.'

'It's what you asked for.'

He nodded. 'That's true. That is true.'

I held out my hands. 'So do we have a deal?'

'On a probationary basis to begin with. Looking at your CV there, you come across as someone with itchy feet. I want to know you aren't going to take off one day because the mood has suddenly come over you.'

'Fair enough.'

'I'm starting you on the salary of a student right out of college and we'll see how you fare. That's my best offer.'

'I'll take it,' I said, and we shook.

The school and the newspaper were to be my life for the next two years.

1

Millie and I stayed at the hotel for another week, which is as long as it took me to find us a small bungalow at the coast end of Garshaigh. Jeff McKinney watched from the window of the bar as I packed our meagre belongings into the Austin. I half expected to see him hanging about outside our new lodgings, but he was, thankfully, nowhere to be seen.

It took me all of forty-five minutes to move in, after which I sat in the kitchen at the rickety chipboard table the landlord had thoughtfully provided and wrote a list of all the things I would now have to buy to make our new residence even semi-functional – most of these missing items I had, of course, left behind when I fled my previous home. This made me feel not a little bit ridiculous, but that was something I was getting more and more used to the older I got, so I shoved the sensation aside and just got on with it.

The house had a tiny garden: a postage-stamp-sized patch of grass surrounded by a sturdy, high wooden fence, so I left Millie to sunbathe out there while I went and bought most of the odds and ends on my list, as well as enough groceries to stock up the fridge and make the place seem a little bit more accommodating. When this was all done I sat on the couch in the Spartan living room and looked at the wall. It looked back. I knew that I should get up and do something – maybe go for a walk, or take my instruments out and give them a clean, perhaps change some strings.

I knew I should, but I just couldn't work up the impetus to move. So I didn't.

I opened my eyes some time later and knew from the texture of light that it was getting towards evening. I had slept most of the day, and felt sluggish and slightly ill. As I shifted on the lumpy couch I realized that my phone was ringing – it was clearly what had woken me. I stood up awkwardly and stumbled into the empty, detergent-smelling kitchen, catching the call just before it went to voicemail.

'Mr Dunphy.' The words were barked into the phone almost like an accusation. In my still sleep-addled state, I almost recoiled in shock.

'Uh . . . um . . . who is this please?'

'George Taylor. I'm calling about your night classes.'

I recalled the grey man who ran the local secondary school.

'Oh, yes. Of course. How can I help you Mr Taylor?'

'I have some paperwork for you – your syllabus, students, a calendar for the year – school holidays and such. I thought you might wish to come by and pick them up.'

'What time is it?' I asked, realizing that I usually used my phone to check the hour, and that it was pressed to my ear.

'It is a quarter to five almost precisely. I'm here for another fifteen minutes. After that I will be convening to my bridge club.'

'Bridge?' My brain was still not really performing to par.

'The game of the cultured man, wouldn't you agree?'

I paused for a moment. I didn't know much about bridge, other than it having some vague connection in my head with the actor Omar Sharif.

26

'I'll come right over,' I said, finally, deciding not to pursue the bridge conversation any further. 'Thanks for waiting.'

He hung up without further ado, or the nicety of a 'good-bye'. I, however, did extend the courtesy to Millie, who repaid it by sneezing noisily and then curling up in the warm spot I had just vacated on the couch. Maybe I could learn something from George Taylor.

He did not get up when I was shown in to his office. The desk he sat behind was an enormous, oaken affair with various files, books and odds and ends organized carefully along the edge. Probably alphabetically, or by date, perhaps. Without looking up from the page he was reading, a red pen poised in his right hand, he gestured with his left at a chair by the wall. It wasn't in front of the desk, but slightly to the side, as if the occupant was not meant to be the centre of attention – more an after-thought. But there was nowhere else to sit, and I didn't fancy standing awkwardly while my new boss decided he was ready to speak to me, so I did as instructed and twiddled my thumbs.

'Your references are all very good, Mr Dunphy,' George Taylor said, his head still bowed to his work.

'I know,' I said. 'That's why I use them. I have found that being bad-mouthed by former employers does not serve me well when job hunting.'

George Taylor's head rose slowly to look at me.

'Are you mocking me, Mr Dunphy?'

I grinned.

'Mr Taylor, I have the unseemly habit of finding myself amusing from time to time. When this happens, I tend to feel the need to share my humorous observations with those around me. Please forgive me.'

Taylor blinked, as if what I had just said had been in a for-eign language.

'Well . . . yes . . . quite. A gentleman named Benjamin Tyrrell whom I spoke to said you could be a bit of a wit.'

'Ben said I could be a bit of a wit?'

'Those were not his exact words.'

'No?'

'I believe he said you could be a "pain in the arse" and that you "thought yourself far funnier than you were". He also said you were one of the most talented people he had ever worked with.'

'Well, the first part sounds like him.'

George Taylor put down his pen and opened a drawer, taking out a thick grey cardboard folder. He handed it to me.

'The course we run here is the standard professional qualification in childcare – the FETAC Level 5 certificate. This contains eight modules, four of which you will teach the groups this year, four next year. Starting one week from today, you will commence tutoring your students in Child Development, Professional Practice in Childcare, Physical Care of the Child and Early Childhood Education. The remaining four will be addressed in the following academic year.'

'Seems pretty straightforward,' I said.

'You will find the syllabi for all modules in your folder, as well as the names of your students, broken down into two classes, one which you will take from 7 until 9.30 on a Tuesday evening, one for the same duration on a Thursday. The classrooms you will be using are detailed therein, and you will also see that I have included a map of the building and its surrounding grounds. Any support equipment you may need – photocopiers, computers, computer disks, whiteboard markers and dusters – is available here, and you have a list of where to locate everything in your pack too. Tea, coffee and a selection of biscuits will be available in the staffroom on your first evening, but the usual custom is for staff to operate a kitty to keep supplies replenished.'

'Fair enough.'

'Do you have any questions, Mr Dunphy?'

'You have made everything admirably clear,' I said. 'Is there anything further you would like to ask me?'

'Would you consider cutting your hair and shaving your beard? If you pardon my saying so, you do not look like a teacher, and the school has a reputation to uphold.'

I smiled. I had wondered if this was going to come up. The older I got, the less often people took offence at my appearance, but George Taylor struck me as a big fish in a very small pond. He was used to being the headmaster, not just of the school, but of the entire town – I would be prepared to bet good money that he had either taught or been principal to three-quarters of the people living in Garshaigh. I was under no illusions that he was only taking me on out of desperation. I would never have been his first choice, a blow-in who had never been a pupil in his school and chose to affect such a shameful, scruffy appearance.

'You know, Mr Taylor, because you have been through my CV with a fine-tooth comb, that I have had a long career, working for many different agencies, often at management level. I have looked like this since I was in college, give or take some grey hairs and a few spare pounds. I'm a good teacher. I can assure you that your students will be happy and well informed. But no, sir, I will not be going to the barbers, nor will I be taking a razor to my whiskers. You recruit me to the staff of your night school and you do so despite my appearance, windswept and interesting though it may be.'

George Taylor sighed deeply.

'I see,' he said. 'Well, I cannot be condemned for raising the issue. I may raise it again at a future juncture.'

'The result will be the same,' I said. 'And if we are to be working together, would you please call me Shane?'

The grey man nodded briskly. 'So be it. You may continue calling me Mr Taylor. Now, I must away to my bridge club. If you have any difficulties, please call me immediately. It is essential we make a good impression on the first night. Mature students can be very difficult.'

'I'll be sure to do so,' I said as he ushered me out the door, closing it behind me and taking his leave once again without a goodbye or a thank you. Shaking my head in exasperation, I walked back to my new home through the growing shadows of the early evening.

The girl was sitting beside me on a bank of grass overlooking a field of buttercups. We were reading a storybook, *Beauty and the Beast*, although I was doing all the reading. My companion contributed by commenting on the pictures.

'Her gots a *beautiful* dress. Lookie that. Is blue, that dress.'

I had noticed she seemed to have only the one dress, of indistinct grey/white.

'Do you like blue dresses?'

'I like blue an' red an' lellow an' pink an' green' an' purpural an' norange an' . . . an all dem colours!'

'Why don't you ask your mum or dad to get you one?'

'Daddy says you shouldn' oughta spend you money. Tha's how you keep whats you got an' gets more.'

'By never buying anything?'

'Show me nudder picture.'

I turned over the page. The Beast, who looked like a cross between a goat and an ape, was leering at the terrified Beauty. He was dressed in a black cape and a pair of dark leggings.

'Him scary,' the girl observed.

'He is. But sometimes he's nice, isn't he? See, here, Beauty has gone into a room she's been told not to. So I think he's mad. He has been nice to her though, mostly.'

The girl ran her finger gently over the picture.

'Maybe there a Good Beast an' a Bad Beast.'
'Maybe.'
'I know someone like dat.'
'Do you?'
'Show me nudder picture!'

2

Robert Chaplin was driving his 1990 Volkswagen Golf down a narrow country lane that looked to me as if it hadn't seen much traffic for a very long time.

'The Blaneys are well known around Garshaigh,' he said, a cigarette dangling from his lower lip as if it were stuck on. 'Tom Blaney, the paterfamilias, is the next to last in a line of thugs, gangsters and dodgy dealers going back to the fucking Norman invasion. He still has ideas about himself and his entitlements, but he is about the only person hereabouts who does. Tom is built like a shithouse wall and has about as much charm. He is ignorant, low minded, vicious and evil, and he would think absolutely nothing of beating you to a pulp and dumping you in a bog hole somewhere. He doesn't look like much, Shane, but please, take my word for it: do not underestimate him, and never turn your back on him.'

'He *did* invite us out here, didn't he?' I asked as a wide field of corn opened up to my left.

'He did, but that means nothing,' Chaplin said.

'You said he was the next to last in his familial line.'

'I did. The Blaneys have always had money, and lots of it. It came here from England and France in the warships that brought Strongbow and his people here a thousand years ago.'

'You think their money's that old?'

'I know it is. I'm the editor of a local newspaper in a small town in which almost nothing of gravity ever happens. One of the few interesting things for a hack like me to do is Blaney watching. I've spent a long time researching them, and I can assure you, my young friend, their money still has sand on it from the fucking crusades.'

'So Tom is rich.'

'No. Well, sort of, I suppose. See all this land?'

I glanced about. We were driving through a huge expanse of what seemed to be farmland, although most of it was lying fallow, generally untended and overgrown.

'I see it.'

'This is all Tom's. Fifty acres. He inherited the lot – it was granted to the Blaneys in one of the early medieval charters and has never been out of their coffers.'

'It doesn't look like it's being treated with love, exactly,' I observed.

'Tom is not a great farmer. And over the past ten years or so he has developed some strange ways.'

'Yeah?'

'You'll see. I don't want to ruin it for you.'

The lane wound on through the flat landscape, sometimes punctuated by a grove of trees or a standing stone. At times I could see the ocean, and with the window rolled down slightly I could smell it, too, a sharp undercurrent of salt behind the wind. It was a wild, untouched kind of place, and I did not find it difficult to imagine medieval farmers tending the land with huge, shaggy cattle lumbering about them, tearing the tough scutch grass from the ground with flat, blunt teeth.

'And Tom and his family live out here?' I said. 'We're at least a mile from the road to town.'

'Closer to two,' Chaplin said. 'You're gonna be walking for an hour if you want to get back to civilization. But Tom rarely does. Here we are.'

We rounded a corner and there, rising out of the earth like a monolith was a huge, brown stone house that seemed to grow out of the harsh country rather than having been built by human hands. The roof, once made of red slate, had over the years sprouted a healthy crop of moss which was now green and glistening. Here and there patches of high reeds reached skywards as if they were waiting for someone to pull them free. The structure itself looked as if it had been built in various stages over many hundreds of years – one corner looked as if it was an original Norman castellum, and was now all but in ruins. Other wings could have dated from any time during the past two centuries, windows seemingly punched into the walls with little or no thought as to how the external facade would look. Some blocks of the construction were a good four floors in height, while others were one. I spied a gate opening onto a flight of stairs running below ground, and surmised that the dwelling also had some subterranean rooms.

It was, in all, one of the most muddled, jumbled constructions I had ever seen.

Chaplin pulled up right outside a large door that had once been painted red but was now a cracked, peeling rusty brown, much like the rest of the building.

'Here we go,' he said, reaching across me to pull a notebook and a couple of pens out of the glove compartment. 'You've got an audio recorder on your phone?'

'Yup.'

'Great. Obviously we need his permission to use it, but be ready to roll when I give you the nod. During the interview,

I don't want you to say anything, okay? Tom is really easily riled, and I'm used to him. I need you to listen, observe and we'll pool our thoughts when we get back to the office.'

'You still haven't really told me why we're here,' I said.

'I want you to come to it as fresh as possible. The whole Blaney thing is really fucking complicated – there's so much history and such a hell of a lot of bitterness, coming from inside the family itself and directed at the family from outside – see, I'm not a hundred per cent certain I can stay completely objective.'

'So that's why you brought me along. An outside ear.'

'Exactly. I'll more than likely write this one up myself – the Blaneys have been a project of mine for a lot of years now. But I want your take on it as a comparison.'

'Right you be,' I said. 'Let's go and see what the story is.'

Chaplin knocked and as we waited I checked the new phone I had bought when I'd gotten the gig at *The Western News*. It was one of those fancy, touch-screen jobs that were all the rage (and which I did not have a great deal of fondness for), but it had a data storage capacity greater than most computers and a voice recorder app that was as good as most professional digital sound studios. It was also small and inconspicuous, and therefore unlikely to cause any undue alarm. Satisfied that it was working, I set it to begin recording at a single touch, slipped a wireless earphone into my left ear and put the phone back in my pocket.

The door was opened by a large, dark-haired, stubble-faced man dressed in a stained grey shirt, tatty jeans and sandals with odd socks. He was perhaps five feet eleven in height with wide shoulders and a startlingly pronounced gut.

'Tom, hello. You asked me to come out for a chat,' Chaplin said, not offering his hand. 'This is the new fella, Shane Dunphy.'

Tom said nothing, but scrutinized me sourly. After a few seconds he stepped back to allow us entry.

The house was surprisingly dark. As we walked a long, narrow hallway, I noticed that there were light fittings at regular intervals above us, but that none contained bulbs. The passage opened onto a high-ceilinged room, that seemed to be a general living area – I noted some books lying here and there, a few ancient children's toys and a couple of unwashed coffee mugs. The floor was scuffed, well-worn wood, the walls bare plaster. Tom motioned to a couch that looked as if it might be homemade: wooden beams nailed together and loosely stuffed pillows, their covers made of rough wool. We sat.

'You've pissed me off in the past,' were the first words our host said as he pulled up a wooden stool and sat heavily down on it, leaning his elbows onto his knees.

'You're easily annoyed, Tom,' Chaplin said, taking out his box of cigarettes and offering them about. Tom took one, I shook my head.

'You're as attracted to fiction as you are to the truth,' Tom said when his smoke was lit.

'Where you and your brood are concerned, it's often hard to tell the difference.'

'I called you out here to tell you the truth. The truth about events that could destroy the Blaney family in these parts – maybe forever.'

Chaplin shrugged. 'Maybe that would be a good thing. Maybe it would please me better to let ye eat yourselves up. Quietly, so as no one would ever get wind of it. God knows, you've done enough damage to Garshaigh and its people to deserve such a fate.'

Tom eyed my boss warily. 'Do you want to hear my story or not?'

37

'You go on the record, fully. You sign a release to say that you agreed to us recording what you say, and you do not go on local radio or talk to that fucking free advertiser they give out in the supermarket saying I misquoted you.'

Tom nodded.

Chaplin looked at me rapidly, and took out his pen. I tapped the phone in my pocket, and heard the earphone hiss into life. We were recording.

'All right. If you have a story I think is worth writing, I'll publish it. So go on: talk.'

Tom Blaney settled himself and took a breath. I got the sense that he had rehearsed what he was about to say.

'You know that this land has been in my family for hundreds of years. The house and the land it is on were left to me by my father, and they were left to him by his father and so on back into the mists of time: father to eldest son. As it should be.'

He drew on the cigarette and exhaled smoke through his nose.

'I have tried to treat it with respect – the land. I work it using the old methods: no chemicals, no heavy machines. I live in this house with my family as generations have done before me – I light the house with candles we make in a workshop out back. I heat it with wood I take from the sea or cut myself from the ditches. I build my own furniture, I grow or kill my own food. I draw water from my own well to drink, cook with and wash in. My family is *connected* to the land, Mr Chaplin. It is in our blood.'

I listened carefully. If I was interpreting it correctly, Tom Blaney was saying that he did not use electricity, and that the house did not have running water. They seemed to be operating a self-sufficient lifestyle. I felt a surge of admiration – such a path was not easy to walk.

Then something caught my eye.

38

Somewhere down the back of the long room I sensed move-ment. I peered through the gloom – the windows in this part of the rambling house were small and high up – yes, I was right: a head of blonde curls peeped over the top of a chair and ducked out of sight. We were being watched.

'I always believed that I would pass the estate on to my eldest boy, Jim, when the time came. I never thought for one second that anyone would try and take away my son's birth-right. And if such a thought had crossed my mind, the notion that the person who would attempt such an act of barbarity would be my own brother would have been so foreign as to be laughable.'

'But that's what has happened?' Chaplin coaxed him on.

'Yes.'

The blonde curls had crept closer. I could see now that they sat atop the head of a girl who looked to be five or six. She was dressed in a shapeless, colourless shift dress and was barefoot. I did not make any sign that I had seen her. I could tell that the game she was playing was all about sneaking up on us without being detected.

'You know my brother, Gerry,' Tom said.

'Everyone living hereabouts knows Gerry,' Chaplin said. 'He's on the local council, he runs half a dozen very profit-able businesses, he sits on just about every society going, from the Masons to the school board . . . so he's trying to buy the land?'

'It's not so simple. If he were just trying to buy it I would say no and that would be that.'

'So what is happening then?'

'There are moves afoot to build a large development on the coastline – shops, a hotel, a cinema, a huge car park.'

'Yes, I sent my man here out to cover a meeting of the pro-test group last week.'

'Gerry has done some deal with the developers, told them he can get me to sell so they can start their work on this land rather than the bog they set their sights on – he seems to think local opinion will be less hostile to them uprooting me and my brood.'

'He can't make you,' Chaplin said. 'Tell him to sling his hook.'

'He's contesting my right to hold the land. He has produced some document that indicates my father was not of sound mind when he passed the estate to me. Which means he can look for the lot to be sold and the proceeds divided.'

Blondie was now crouched behind some sort of narrow table, on top of which a lumpy, homemade vase of marsh flowers sat unevenly. She grinned at me when I tried to steal a look at her, and put her fingers to her lips: *sshhh!*

'Well, that's a legal matter,' Tom said. 'Not really a case for the newspaper.'

'They have tried to intimidate us out. There have been people skulking about the fields, threatening my wife. Scaring the children. You know what Gerry can be like.'

Chaplin considered that. 'I do. But then, he's cut from the same cloth as you. You're not above coming into a man's offices and threatening to break up his already virtually obsolete equipment when he prints an opinion piece you don't like.'

'I never have and never would target your family. If he was just coming after me, I wouldn't mind.'

Chaplin pursed his lips and thought about this information. 'When was the last time he sent someone out?'

'It's almost a daily occurrence.'

'You understand that I can't accuse a prominent businessman or a large multinational company of threats and intimidation without evidence.'

'I don't own a phone or a camera or even a television set,' Blaney said. 'What evidence are you looking for?'

'I'd like to leave my associate here for the day. If anything happens, he'll be here, can testify to the truth of your claims. And that, you see, is evidence.'

'He can stay so long as he doesn't get in the way.'

'I'll be the soul of discretion,' I said ruefully.

The blonde child had begun her creep back across the room, unseen by my two companions. I watched her until she disappeared into the murk.

3

I discovered that the child's name was Emma, and she was
ten. I sat at a rough-hewn table in the kitchen while Dora,
Tom's wife, cut thick slices of home-baked brown bread,
with the child perched opposite me. Dora was a doughty,
broad woman, physically very like her husband, with a thick
frizz of strawberry-blonde hair that was almost an afro. Her
hands were like shovels. Next to her was a small red-haired
boy, Dom, who was twelve but looked perhaps eight, and
an auburn-haired girl, Winnie, who was thirteen but looked
ten. There was another boy, Jim, whom Tom had referred to
during our conversation, but he had gone off with his father
to scout the perimeter for intruders. They refused to allow me
to go with them, stating that they would bring any interlopers
back with them. There wasn't much to say to that, so I had
waited with the children and Dora.

It was immediately clear that what Tom Blaney claimed
about their lifestyle was true: they most certainly did not use
either electricity or running water. Dora had a pump installed
over a deep metal sink, and she gave it one or two vigorous
tugs if she needed water. A huge solid-fuel stove burned on the
back wall, and she intermittently added a block of wood to it.

'I hope you don't mind my saying, Mrs Blaney, but I'm fascinated by your decision to live in such a . . . uh . . . a traditional way. It must be very challenging.'

'It wasn't my decision,' she said, banging the plate of bread down in front of me. 'Tom Blaney is a stubborn man, and he and his father developed this notion of living in a way that would make their forefathers proud or some such nonsense. I'd kill for a washing machine and drier. But he won't hear of it.'

The children watched us, following the conversation wide-eyed. I stuck my tongue out at Emma. She wrinkled her nose in a rude face.

'To be honest, there's a story just in the way you live from day to day,' I said. 'It would certainly put things in perspective – do you know that I come across people who couldn't imagine going a day without Facebook, let alone without electricity altogether.'

'Emma there is our youngest,' Dora said, setting a plate of cured ham and a glass of buttermilk in front of me. 'She has never seen a television, except the ones in the shop windows on the rare occasions we go into town. She has never hit a switch and had a light come on, and she has never eaten a meal cooked on an electric hob.'

I looked at the tiny child, who was spreading butter onto her bread from a block in the middle of the table. This little girl had never watched MTV, had no experience of the radio or of mobile phones. Sitting there with her ringlets and her huge blue eyes, it was as if I had been beamed into the past by magic. She was a child from the past – a girl from yesterday.

'So you had to learn how to use all this retro kitchen equipment?'

'I did. It's actually not as difficult as you'd think. The oven cooks much quicker than a gas or electric one. You just have to learn how to control the heat. It's all about piling up the coals at various points. But you get the hang of it by trial and error.'

The bread was very good, as was the meat – salty and sweet all at once. I generally don't drink milk, but I actually do like buttermilk, so I had a hearty lunch. The children all remained completely silent, but I chatted at them and continued to pull silly faces and generally try to make friends. It was nice to be able to do so without the added responsibility of knowing I might have to take them into care, and I just relaxed and had fun.

They were a strange lot, all dressed in their drab, sagging clothes, all very small for their age and more than a little grubby. But these were simply observations. I figured that I would probably be more than a little dirty too if I had no running water and the only way to heat what water I did have was to put it in a large pot over the fire.

I drained my glass and banged it down on the table.

All the children jumped as if I had fired a gun: they froze for a second, seemingly waiting for me to do something even more threatening. Of course, I had frozen too, alarmed at *their* reaction. When I did nothing, Emma started to laugh, almost hysterically. I joined in, more out of discomfort than anything else. Such a startle reflex usually meant a rather volatile home environment, but then Chaplin had told me that Tom was a bit of a thug.

Dora sent the children out to play and I insisted on helping with what little washing up there was, more to get a chance to talk to her away from the kids than anything else.

'These intruders,' I said. 'Have you been frightened by them?'

'I haven't seen any,' she said. 'I'm inside the house mostly, but Tom has seen them, and so have the kids. It scares me that they're out there, looking to do us harm.'

'What have they threatened to do?'

'To hurt us.'

'How?'

She paused, drying up a mug.

'I don't really know. Tom has been dealing with them.'

I continued to wash the cutlery in the virtually cold water.

'And would you like to move? Sell up?'

She sighed and leaned her back against the draining board. She was about ten years younger than her husband and seemed educated. I got the sense that a lot of the joy in life had been taken from her.

'When I married Tom, I knew I was marrying a Blaney. He was quite a catch in those days. But of course I had no idea what I was getting myself in to. I thought I was going to get a nice chunk of money and land and maybe a little respect locally. But sure he's the 'weird' brother. The strange one. Gerry, he would have been the *real* catch, but sure I was a fool. I'll be straight with you – I hate this house, I hate the land and I'm none too fond of the Blaney legacy, neither. It's brought me nothing but pain. Would I sell up? You'd better believe I would, in a heartbeat.'

'But all the history . . .'

'When I got married first, I tried to go through all the papers. There are literally rooms and rooms of them out back. I spent months on it, and I thought Tom would be thrilled. You know what he told me? He said the legacy, the history, is all in his head and in his heart. He didn't need any documents or papers to preserve it.'

We finished the washing up in silence. I wanted to take a walk around the land, but I was well aware that if I did and someone showed up intent on intimidating the family I could not be contacted – I was the only one with a mobile phone.

45

'Your house is really amazing,' I said as we put the last mug away. 'Is it as old as it looks?'

'The first section was built in the twelfth century,' Dora said, 'or so Tom says. It's been added on to in dribs and drabs since then as various Blaneys decided they required extra space. To be honest, we only live in the living room, which you've seen, the kitchen, and three bedrooms directly above. The rest is in a fair state of disarray. It drives Tom nuts, but then, he isn't prepared to clean it.'

'Can I have a look around? I'm kind of a history buff.'

'If you want to.'

'I won't poke about. I just think the building is really unique.'

'Oh, it's surely that all right.'

I spent the next hour wandering about what proved to be a much bigger superstructure than I had at first realized. I had a vague sense as I passed from one ruined ramshackle section to another of the time frames they had been built in, but only in a very loose way. The rooms currently occupied seemed to have been finished in the 1960s or thereabouts, and adjoining these was a series I reckoned dated back to the 1880s – at this stage it seemed the Blaneys were less concerned about the onslaught of technology as, on an old office stand, I found an ancient wireless radio. In this part of the house also were outlets for gas lamps still attached to the walls. Black and white photographs showed faces with strong familial likenesses to Tom and the children: a man leaning against a plough, another with his arm about the neck of a huge horse; a sad-eyed woman in a ball gown gazing into the camera, a swarthy, heavily moustached man beside her; a child of indeterminate gender dressed in what looked like a white dress, his/her arm resting on a spaniel dog. I found an attic room filled with toys of varying ages, children's annuals dating back to the

Victorian era and a pianoforte that was at least 200 years old and desperately out of tune. In one of the basements, using the light from my fancy new phone, I found an old church, complete with rows of pews, an altar made from rocks taken from the wild fields about the house itself and a huge crucifix above the stone table carved from local bog oak, burnished by hand.

Finally I came out into the section that was the oldest, clearly an ancient castle house built by the Blaney who'd sailed here with his mercenary colleagues back in the days when Celtic tribes still walked the land hereabouts and the Vikings had just settled in my own native Wexford. I stood on the second floor, which was just about safe, made as it was of thick wooden planks set into grooves in the stone. One of the windows had started to crumble at the edge, creating a large hole through which I could see the land right down to the sea. I took a deep breath, feeling the wind on my face. It was pleasant after spending so long in the dust and dark of the ruined estate. A soft footfall made me turn, and there was Emma, the blonde, ringleted youngest of the family.

'Hey,' I said. 'Have you been following me?'

The little girl nodded.

'For long?'

No reaction to that. Just wide eyes as she leaned against the rough stone of the doorway.

'You live in a strange and beautiful place, Emma,' I said. 'All this space and so much history. Your family have lived and worked and played and died on this very spot for close to a thousand years.'

'It is . . . who we are,' the little voice was quiet and halting, but I could make out what she said very clearly.

'It is who you are,' I repeated, turning to her. 'Does your dad say that?'

She nodded, seemingly embarrassed by having spoken.

'Well, I reckon that is a very good way of thinking about it. This place *is* who you are in a lot of ways.'

Emma, in tiny, skittering steps, came from the door to stand beside me.

'Where is the place that is who you are?' she asked as we both gazed out over her homestead.

I laughed.

'D'you know what, sweetie? I have no idea.'

She tutted and shook her head.

'Your home!' she said. 'Where is that?'

She had little accent, but her voice had a sweet, musical quality that was very pleasant to listen to. In the light of early afternoon, I could see that beneath the mop of hair she was extremely pretty.

'Right now my home is a rather horrible little house in Garshaigh. Before that it was a cottage far away from here. Where it will be next, I don't know.'

The girl tutted and shook her head, as if I was speaking terrible nonsense. Suddenly, I sensed her tense.

'Look!' she said, pointing at a spot on the horizon. I gazed in the direction she indicated and there, coming down the lane I had traversed with Chaplin that morning, was a green jeep.

'Strangers,' Emma said, turning and disappearing into the dark of the house. 'They come to run us off.'

I followed her at a run.

4

They stopped half a mile up the road and got out of the jeep, four of them walking towards the house, each carrying an axe handle or a hurley. Tom Blaney met them before they had covered half the distance, his eldest son Jim at his side. Tom had a shotgun in his hand, Jim an old-fashioned shillelagh, its vicious blunt head weighted with lead.

I lurked about ten yards behind them, standing a little off to the side, hoping rather pathetically that I might not be seen if things got nasty (though still close enough to hear what was being said).

'I'm asking ye to stop right where ye are, lads,' Tom Blaney said, cocking his gun loudly.

'That's not very hospitable,' the man second from the left said. He was tallest and widest and had a mean, pug-faced look that spoke of little intelligence, and suggested that the small amount there was tended to be focused on meanness and cruelty.

'I offer hospitality to those I invite onto my land, not those who arrive uninvited,' Tom said. 'Now, I know you've come to urge me and mine to leave, I know you are going to suggest that harm will come to us if we don't, and I gather from the fact that you've brought weapons with you that you have every intention of inflicting some of that harm yourselves.'

'He sure do talk nice,' the man on the far right of the group said. He was little more than five feet in height, but was about the same across, his head shaved tight and a livid scar crossing his face in a garish zigzag. 'I think I'm a gonna shut 'im up.'

Tom lowered his gun in an assured, languid movement, as if he cared little either way what happened next, but the tension in the air jumped up a notch, and suddenly it was as if I could feel static in my hair.

'You move one inch, boy, and I'll make a hole in you,' Tom said, the tone of his voice unchanged.

'You're awful jumpy,' the first man said. 'Someone could get hurt with you wavin' that firearm about the place. God knows, could even be your young lad there.'

The sound of the shotgun going off was like someone had punched a gap in existence: it was a sort of crunch, and time imploded for a second. The four men dived in slow motion in varying directions, all desperately trying to avoid the deadly hail coming their way. I (to my shame) let out a little squeal and took two or three steps backwards, then sat down hard.

When time began to speed up again, Tom was still standing right where he was, and the four interlopers were all lying in various undignified positions here and there. The dirt about three feet in front of where they had been standing was all chewed up – Tom had clearly aimed to miss.

'That was one barrel I unloaded,' he said. 'Which means I have a full one here should I choose to use it. Now, Jim,' to his son, who had not even flinched during the shooting, 'I want you to go over to that man who said you might get hurt, and punch him in his head.'

'He comes within arm's reach of me and I'm gonna floor him,' the subject of this instruction said, although it is difficult to sound tough when you are sprawled in the weeds.

'You so much as raise a hand against him and I will hit you directly in the gut, which will not kill you outright, but will leave you in agonizing pain as you bleed to death slowly. Go on now, Jim. Give him a good thump. He needs to be shown that you do not insult or threaten a Blaney.'

Jim nodded and walked solemnly up to the man, drew back his fist and delivered a punch directly to the top of his head. I could hear the pop from where I still sat on the ground. The man groaned and sagged for a moment, stunned and disoriented.

'Good boy, Jimbo,' Tom Blaney said. He walked up to where the men were struggling to get on their feet. 'Now, gentlemen, would you be so good as to go back to my brother and tell him that I have no intention at all of leaving my home, and that if he has anything else to say, to be man enough to come down here and say it himself? The quality of help he's sendin' is pretty damned awful anyway.'

Helping their still stunned comrade to his feet, the gang of four unsteadily made their way back to the jeep. Tom watched as it turned and drove away.

'You did good, Jim,' he said. 'He won't forget you in a hurry. The next time he comes across you, he'll know you can throw a punch. That makes a difference.'

He turned to me.

'You seen enough, longhair?'

'I have,' I said.

'Well why don't you go on and tell your boss that I am not a fantasist, then.'

'I will,' I said. 'I just need to ring for a cab.'

'Jim here will run you into town.'

51

I nodded and followed the boy to the ancient Range Rover the family used, which was parked by the front door.

'I have one question, Mr Blaney, before I go,' I said.

He paused, his back still to me.

'What did you do to your brother to make him *so* pissed off at you?'

Tom Blaney stayed frozen for a second, then continued walking.

'Goodbye Mr Dunphy,' he said, 'please send my regards to your employer.'

Jim drove me back to Garshaigh in silence.

5

The first evening of my night classes was upon me before I knew it. I had spent hours looking over the modules I would be covering and refamiliarizing myself with the finer points of the ideas, concepts and practical activities I would be delivering to my groups.

For the first night I determined to make George Taylor happy by dressing a little smarter than usual, so I dug out a shirt and ironed it, polished my shoes and made sure my hair was at least slightly under control for a change.

'What do you think?' I asked Millie, standing before her in all my finery. 'Do I look like someone you would listen to? When you see me do you think "educator"?'

Millie looked me over with a bored expression and gave a rough bark that seemed non-committal. I felt she was trying to avoid giving me a definitive answer.

There was nothing to be gained by arguing with an evasive greyhound, so I packed my laptop into my shoulder bag and strolled the short distance to the school.

George Taylor had requested that I arrive an hour early, to give me a chance to get set up so that when the students arrived I could begin orientation immediately. He was buzzing about in the reception area when I came in, looking anxious and bothered.

'Good, good, you're here,' he said.

'I am,' I agreed.

'Do you require any photocopying to be done, or any other equipment to be in place?'

'No,' I said. 'I think I have everything under control.'

'You think?' George Taylor said tersely. 'I do not like people who "think" they are ready.'

'I *know* that I am ready, Mr Taylor, and I would like to go to my classroom now and get everything prepared. The students will, I expect, be arriving within the next forty minutes.'

'Yes. Quite so, quite so,' Taylor said, and buzzed off to annoy someone else.

The map the principal had given me was accurate, but to be safe I had gone to the school the previous week to ensure I could find my way around, and was therefore able to go straight to my class without difficulty. It was a wide, characterless room, unadorned by posters or art of any kind, simply a space filled with tables and chairs, a large whiteboard at the front with a teacher's desk in front of it. Hanging from the ceiling was a PowerPoint projector, and the cable to connect my laptop to it hung down onto a little platform set into the wall. I plugged my computer into the mains, switched it on, stood on a chair to turn on the projector, which made a little singsong noise to let me know it was functional, then plugged the cable running from the projector into the computer. A blue square was being projected onto the whiteboard, but nothing else happened. I hit a couple of keys, enabling my system to be read by the school's network, and in a second my desktop screen was being shown in an enlarged format on the board.

I had an introductory class planned for the first hour, in which I would tell the students what to expect from me and my teaching methods, then there would be coffee, and after that I would get the group to introduce themselves, tell me what they wanted from the course, and hopefully provide the option for some discussion and conversation.

I had taught off and on for quite a few years, and I had my style down pretty well. I felt that teaching, in its most effective form, was a sort of educational stand-up. Many educators believe that they do not need to entertain, that they are purely a delivery system for the information. I can see the logic behind that, I just don't agree with it. I have always found that people learn more when they are engaged, and that people tune in more when they are interested and amused by the topic at hand. I believe that making each lesson as attractive and interesting as possible can only be a positive thing. I hoped that my introduction would set the tone for that.

Foremost on my mind that evening was the need to match my delivery to the needs of the punters I was going to have sitting in front of me, all of whom would be expecting to be enlightened and inspired. Night-class students can be a mixed bunch. I am aware that people sign up for childcare courses for lots of different reasons, and people come to night classes often without the intention of pursuing their chosen subject as anything more than a hobby. I expected to have a group mostly made up of female students, all adults, the vast majority in middle age, who were coming along as much for the social experience as to learn a new set of skills.

I had no problem with that. I like teaching because I think it is important to get the information I teach out there – I harbour the belief that childcare and child protection are essential sciences for the development and progression of our society – and I make no apology for it. But I also enjoy the interaction with my students and the opportunity to learn from them – for me teaching has always been a two-way street. I love hearing their stories, participating in their learning experience and seeing that wonderful moment when the penny drops and they really 'get' a difficult concept or idea. That, for me, is what teaching is all about.

When I was satisfied that the computer and projector were working seamlessly, I chose some music from the vast library I keep on my computer and set it playing gently. I went for recognizable, middle-of-the-road, non-threatening material: Johnny Cash, James Taylor, early Leonard Cohen, Joni Mitchell – I wanted to create a soothing, pleasant atmosphere. I also made a point of turning off most of the lights, so the room was in a comfortable glow – this made it easier to read the images projected onto the board, and also relaxed the learners. While many would bound in, fresh-faced and ready for action, others would be nervous and not a little scared, feeling a dread of the classroom having last spent time in one to do their Leaving Cert. Some not even having gotten that far. I never underestimate the bravery required to sign up for a night class. I wanted to make the experience as easy as possible for each and every member of the group – those happy to be returning to learning, and those there against their better judgement.

Class was due to begin at seven, but as I had predicted the first student – a woman in her late twenties with short hair dyed purple – came in, looking about her meekly, at twenty minutes to the hour. I was by then seated at the teacher's desk with my feet up on it, reading a Lee Child novel. I smiled and nodded, invited her to sit, but did no more than that. I felt it was important that everyone find their own feet, and I did not want to engage the group in small talk before class began. The dynamic was different than in a college or a school, and I was very conscious of the fact that I would have to grade assignments and class work. Therefore, I was not and could not be their friend. It did no harm to keep a little bit of a distance.

The room filled up, slowly at first, but gradually the flow of bodies came quicker and quicker. Of course the seats at the back of the room filled up first, but by five to seven we were pretty much chock-a-block. I checked the time. I would give it right up until seven, but I was determined (as much for the gratification of George Taylor as for my own professionalism) to begin at seven o'clock on the button. I turned the page and began another chapter in the exciting life of Jack Reacher.

There was a gentle, comfortable murmur as I read. The group, which, if everyone showed up, was thirty-eight in number, were a motley bunch – there were four males among them (which pleased me) and a broad cross section of age – one girl was not yet out of her teens, I guessed, while one of the men could have been seventy.

At seven I stood, closed my book and cleared my throat. All chat ceased almost immediately, and eyes turned to the front of the room.

'My name is Shane Dunphy, and I'm going to be teaching you this year as you cover half the modules for your Certificate in Childcare. I'm going to call the register in just a moment, and when I call each of your names, I'd like you to stand up quickly and make yourself known. It'll take me some time to get to know all of you, and the more I connect faces to the names the better.'

There was general discomfort and a few murmurs of unhappiness at this looming exposure, but I didn't give them a chance to dwell on it. I turned the focus back on to myself.

'Okay, so, why am I – a bloke – teaching you a subject that is, let's face it, dominated by women? The statistics for childcare as a profession show us that 90 per cent of all childcare work, both inside and outside the home, is done by women. It's inarguable, and I bet most of you were expecting a female teacher.'

There was some nodding and one or two mutters at this. I smiled.

'Here is my main response to the question,' I said. 'Why a male childcare teacher? Why not? Why shouldn't a guy be as competent in looking after the care and welfare of children as a woman? I am here because I am qualified to be, and also because I have worked in almost every area of childcare and child protection. I've run crèches, I've worked in residential care, I've done community-based child protection work, I've spent time in day centres with adults with intellectual disabilities and I've also worked in the early years with children with special needs. I've worked with the travelling community and with non-Irish nationals. I've done community arts work and I've been in almost every prison in the country – not as a detainee, I hasten to add! So I have some experience to fall back on.'

They were quiet now. I had them. They were listening intently.

'You'll have to make your own minds up about me,' I said. 'But there is one thing I know for certain about all of you. You may be here for different reasons, but you have one thing in common. You are here because you *want to be here*. I have taught on professional courses in colleges and universities, and a lot of those students were there because *their parents* wanted them to be there, not because they really had any interest in the course themselves. You have all taken the initiative to come out in the evening after you've finished work, or when your family have come home, to do this course because you truly feel compelled to know more about children and what makes them tick. And I really admire that. You see, I think childcare is the most important job in the world. In childcare, we go out every day and we ask people to hand over their kids to us for a while. We take parental responsibility for those children – for the future police officers and doctors and petrol pump attendants and teachers and chefs and insurance salesmen – there is no greater thing you could ask anybody to do than allow you to care for their young.'

Murmurs of assent. Some were nodding.

'I take this very seriously, and I'm going to ask you to as well. Now don't get me wrong – we will have a lot of fun, too. But I need you to be prepared to give me a hundred and ten per cent when you are here. I don't care what you do when you're outside these walls – when you come in to me you are childcare workers, and I will treat you the exact same way I treat a team in the field. I expect the same level of profession-alism and the same level of commitment. Okay?'

Enthusiastic nods. Good.

'All right, let's call the register, get to know you a little bit.'

I ran through the list of students, and learned three things: firstly, we were one down – someone named Gladys Pointer had not arrived; secondly, I would never remember all these names – I would have to work hard at learning them; thirdly, Carla, the pretty waitress from the café was among my stu-dents: I was glad to see at least one face I sort of knew. It looked like there was going to be great diversity in terms of confidence and ability: even the simple act of standing up and nodding hello to the group elicited vastly differing reactions – some stood up straight, beamed a smile and said hello in an open, friendly way, others barely lifted themselves from their seats and simply raised a finger in my direction. Still more seemed ready to say a few words about themselves: 'I'm Julianne and I'm really pleased to be here.'

When I had called out the last name I closed the register and stood again, tucking my pen back into my breast pocket.

'I know some of you are glad that's over,' I said (more nodding

SHANE DUNPHY

and some relieved laughter). 'You are all very welcome. Could I have a volunteer to help me with something please?'

No one raised their hand, so I picked out one of the group who had been very anxious to speak during the register and introduction section. It was one of the male students, a guy in his early twenties called Tim Phelan.

'Okay Tim,' I said, leading him to the top of the class. 'Do you have a day job?'

'I do,' he said.

'Tell me about it.'

'Well, I work for a company that sells medical equipment,' he began. 'I always wanted to be a nurse, see, but I didn't get on that well at school . . .'

He stopped, because I had my head bowed, clearly in the middle of texting someone on my mobile phone.

'Carry on,' I said. 'I just have to take this. You work away. I'm listening.'

'Well, I always wanted to do somethin' that involved helpin' people, givin' somethin' back, y'know?'

He stopped again at this point, because I burst out laughing, not at what he'd said but at whatever I was reading in my latest message.

'Oh, sorry, sorry,' I said. 'My bad. Keep going, you're doing great. You wanted to give something back, yeah?'

'That's right yeah. I . . . I had an aunt y'see who was a nurse, and she was real good to me and my family. I remember havin' to go into hospital when I was maybe nine or ten and I was so proud when I saw how the other nurses listened to what she had to say . . .'

He trailed off again because I was now lifting the phone up to the light, shaking it and banging it gently into my palm.

'Sorry Tim,' I said. 'Um . . . has anyone got a charger? I think it's dead.'

60

I played it utterly deadpan. I think at this point they really believed I was intent on continuing my phone antics. I did nothing to change that perception until one of the group, a timid-looking girl at the back of the room, actually did produce a charger. I took it from her and plugged in my phone, which was not really dying at all.

'You can sit down, Tim,' I said. 'Now, what was wrong with that picture?'

'You were rude,' said a girl called Rebecca.

'Was I?' I asked.

'That was really mean,' a woman in the middle of the room said. 'I was getting quite angry with you.'

'Well,' I said, 'you may be right. Yet at various points in the year many among you will do exactly what I just did. You'll do it in a slightly less up-front way – you'll hide the phone under the desk and think I can't see you, but guess what? I can.'

I hit the mouse and an image appeared on the whiteboard. It was a shot of a poster that had been put up in a classroom in an American university by one of the lecturers:

Dear Students,
I know when you're texting.
No one just looks down at their crotch
and smiles.

That got a laugh.

'I don't ask any of you to do what I don't do myself. There may be times in class when I have to take a call. If I need to, I'll bring it outside and come back in as quickly as I can. I promise that my phone will not be constantly ringing during class – if it looks like that might happen I'll switch it off . . .'

At this precise moment the door burst open and a girl in her mid-twenties bustled in, speaking loudly into a phone and carrying a load of shopping bags. I stopped and all eyes in the room turned on her. Many would have been terribly embarrassed at this. Most people would have ended the phone conversation. Or at least apologized. This young lady did none of the aforementioned.

'Yeah, yeah I'm just after gettin' to the college. I'll drop over to you tomorrow. No, she won't be there. No, I'm certain she won't. She will? Fuck off! *Fuck off!* I don't believe you!'

At this juncture I cleared my throat very loudly. She threw me a look that said: *what is your problem?*

'Look, Pansy, I'm gonna haveta split, the *teacher* is givin' me evils. Yeah, call me again, all right? Seeya soon.'

The phone was begrudgingly set down. Smiling, I pulled out the only chair left empty.

'You are Gladys Pointer, I presume?' I said as I settled her into her place.

'You presume right,' she said.

'Shall I take some of these bags and put them down over there out of the way?' I offered.

'I'd prefer to have them right where they are,' Gladys said.

'Right you be. You will have to pardon me if I trample over them in the event of a fire.'

'Okay, move them,' the latecomer said through gritted teeth.

'Thank you, I will,' I said.

The rest of the class went off without event. Gladys's arrival had actually worked as a kind of icebreaker, and by the time we hit eight everyone was in high spirits ready to relax over tea and biscuits. I went along for a few minutes just to broach the issue of setting up a kitty.

I was amazed when I arrived in the tea room with my group to find someone there already: Jeff McKinney had parked his wheelchair in the middle of the floor and was sitting, smiling

a welcome. I wasn't sure what to say, so decided simple polite-
ness would have to suffice.

'Hello Jeff,' I said, shaking his extended hand. 'You working here too, then?'

'No, I'm taking a class.'

There were quite a few others on that night, so I waited for
him to tell me which one. He didn't, though.

'Are you going to introduce me to your students?'

'Of course,' I said, turning to face them. 'This is Jeff, everyone. He's a student here too, so you'll have plenty in common.'

When everyone was settled in and pots of tea and coffee
brewed, I scuttled back to the classroom to rearrange the seats
into a circle for the second hour.

When the group came back I could feel the nervousness
radiating from them, but I didn't care – we had overcome their
inhibitions in the first hour and we would this time too.

'Here's something we will do from time to time,' I said.
'Childcare is all about setting the children we work with at ease,
and part of that is showing them that everyone has a right to
be heard, to have a voice and to express themselves in whatever
way works best for them. There will be days where I will bring
in some of my musical instruments and we will spend an hour
singing.' This met with a mixture of delight and total horror.
'There will be days when I bring in paints and paper or crayons
and we will draw. I will participate fully in everything – there
is nothing that you will be asked to do that I will not do myself.
Today, we are going to start getting your views on a few things,
call it a "getting to know you" session. So, I'm going to begin
by going around to everyone, and I want you first to introduce
yourself, then to say why you have an interest in childcare. Tim,
because I used you as a guinea pig earlier, I'm going to give you
the option to either be the first up, or to go last. If you want to
go last, choose the person to go instead of you now.'

Tim, as I had suspected, did want to go, and he continued the story of his aunt the nurse. It was well into the hour before Gladys Pointer's turn came around.

'Hi everyone, I'm Gladys,' she said. She was maybe five feet two inches in height, slim and well dressed with a fashionable haircut and very high heels. Her coat was belted at the waist, and I realized that she hadn't taken it off despite the warmth of the room. Maybe it would ruin her look.

'So, why are you here, Gladys?'

'I don't know,' she said. 'I mean, I'm gonna fail. I just kinda wanted to give it a go.'

'Why do you say that you'll fail?' I asked, laughing. 'You haven't even been with me a night yet. You should give the course a go for a while before making up your mind.'

'Oh, it's not me that thinks it,' she said. 'It's everyone else. Me teachers always told me I was thick and that I was gonna fail. And they were right about the Leaving Cert. But see, I always liked childcare. I thought maybe if I was int'rested in a subject I might work harder.'

'I'm sure you will,' I said. 'Don't take all that stuff to heart. I don't believe there's any such thing as a "thick" person. Just 'cause school didn't work out doesn't mean this won't.'

'Don't you worry about it,' Gladys said, smiling. 'All we can do is try, right?'

'Yes, absolutely,' I said.

She looked at me for a moment as if I was a well-meaning simpleton.

'I expect I'll be gone by Christmas,' she said gently. 'But it won't be your fault. I'm just not that smart, that's all.'

I didn't know what to say. I was struck by the dichotomy of her incredible confidence side by side with her utter defeatism. I only knew one thing: I was determined that I would do my utmost to make sure she did as well as she could.

6

At the end of the night, as the students were saying goodbye to their new friends and filing out, I called Gladys over. She came loaded down with her recently retrieved bags of shopping.

'So,' I said, 'will we be seeing you again?'

'Yeah. It looks like it might be interesting enough,' she said, eyeing me warily. I could tell that, in her world, teachers of all kinds were the enemy. I could understand the perspective – I'd had enough experience of bad educators to know that their impact can be devastating.

'I think you missed me saying at the start of class that my job is to ensure you have the best time here you possibly can,' I said. 'Teaching at this level isn't about my standing at the top of the room and preaching at you for a couple of hours. I want you to realize that you know a lot of this material already – you've been a child, you've been around kids – I'm going to help you put the proper words and language on some of the ideas, but most of it is locked up in your head already.'

'There's one problem right there,' Gladys said, shifting one of her bags from one hand to another – I wanted to take it from her, but I'd had so much trouble wresting them from her grip before, I thought it might be wiser to leave them. 'I has awful trouble with words. I know what I want to say, I don't know how most of the time. And I sometimes think that my head isn't connected to the rest of me at all. I can have all the knowledge in the world locked up there, but there is no way I'm going to get at it.'

'I can teach you how,' I said, 'when you have a tough time at school, books, learning and so on can become very threatening. Look, we made a good start tonight. I just wanted you to know I heard what you said, and I want us to work hard together to make sure it doesn't come to pass.'

Gladys sighed, shaking her head indulgently, and joined her comrades in their exodus from the room. I busied myself rearranging the furniture into its initial formation, and was packing up my computer when George Taylor knocked and entered.

'How went the night, Shane?'

'Well, I think,' I said. 'We had a full contingency and I believe they'll come back.'

'Excellent. That is what I like to hear. In these times of economic ill-health, we need the night school more than ever. It pays for an awful lot of the basic things we need to run the day school – paper, photocopying toner, even heating oil. It is an essential part of what we do, so it is of the utmost necessity that our students leave happy, informed and ready for more.'

'I had a student this evening,' I said, 'Gladys Pointer. I'm assuming she's local, so she probably attended here as a day student. She's not that old, mid-twenties, I think. Do you remember her?'

'The Pointers are a well-known local family,' Taylor said. 'Farmers. I do remember Gladys, yes. If you have her as a student, you will have your work cut out for you. She was a challenging young woman when she was here. I seem to recollect her failing her final exams quite spectacularly.'

'What went wrong?'

'She did, Shane. That is the only thing that can go wrong when it comes to failing an examination.'

'No,' I said, getting a little impatient. 'Does she have poor literacy skills, is it her concentration, her comprehension . . . where is she falling down academically?'

'I never taught her,' Taylor said. 'I'll find out who did and ask them some discreet questions, if you wish, but she is an adult now, Mr Dunphy. Poking about in her records is not really appropriate.'

I paused. He was right. I was falling back on old habits.

'Maybe I should just work with her a bit and see how I go,' I said. 'Thanks for your offer, though.'

'You are quite welcome,' Taylor said, and breezed out. I finished packing up, switched off the lights and went home. Jeff McKinney was sitting in the car park in the dark as I left. I gave him a wave, but he didn't respond.

7

I took Millie for a walk about the town, smoking a cigar while I did so. Pausing to look in the windows of some of the clothes shops (my wardrobe was still very compromised), I realized that fashion had passed me by. There was no way I was going to purchase most of what I saw on offer in the outlets about Garshaigh. As we strolled homewards, I wondered if I might have got it wrong: maybe fashion had, in fact, passed *Garshaigh* by. I thought a trip to Galway might be called for that weekend.

Back at the house I broke out the Bushmills again and plonked in front of the TV. My viewing options hadn't improved since moving from the hotel. Without a satellite dish I could still only pick up an Irish language station, an advertising channel that seemed to specialize in cleaning products (which I noticed always claimed to do absolutely everything you could require a cleaning product to do, which surely made all the *other* products for sale on the channel obsolete), and the erstwhile 1970s and 80s crime channel. This evening a Perry Mason movie was showing, Raymond Burr growling at bad guys in the courtroom.

I'd only had a couple of glasses when Lonnie spoke up from the armchair in the corner.

'Good to see you've moved into a decent place . . . . sort of.'

'Where've you been?' I asked. 'I could've used the help moving in.'

'What, to help you carry your one suitcase? I think you were able to manage that by yourself.'

I grinned and nudged the bottle towards him.

'I actually have a spare glass this time,' I said. 'Under the sink.'

I heard him moving about and then he reached over and took the whiskey, pouring a generous shot for himself.

'So I see you're gainfully employed.'

'Two jobs,' I said. 'I'm gainfully employed twice.'

'Isn't that because both jobs pay you hardly anything at all?'

'It is, but it's not polite to mention that.'

'Okay,' Lonnie said. 'I won't bring it up again.'

'You know, Perry Mason was a little before my time,' I said. 'But this isn't bad.'

'Has it occurred to you that you may be developing a form of Stockholm Syndrome?'

'How do you mean?'

'You're starting to identify with your captors. The TV in this town is so fucking bad, you're forcing yourself to develop a taste for it. Out of desperation. It's a survival mechanism, and I understand why you're giving in.'

'Come on,' I said, laughing at his hypothesis. 'It's not that bad . . .'

'Shane, they show daytime TV all day!' he said. 'What could be worse than that?'

We both erupted into laughter at the good of it.

'They had a *Mannix* weekend,' I said barely able to speak from the laughing. 'I watched three hours of it – back to back! I thought I was going to go crazy!'

'You're talking to a dead dwarf,' Lonnie said. 'I think you *are* crazy!'

We laughed even harder at that. When we finally calmed down I poured us both more drinks and sat back to watch the movie. Except Lonnie had other ideas.

'I've come to talk to you about something.'

'Lonnie, it's really great to see you, but do you always have to arrive full of weighty import? Can't you just drop by like you used to?'

'Shut up and listen to me. You were out at the Blaney place the other day.'

'So?'

'Anything occur to you while you were out there?'

'Well they're pretty damned weird, if that's what you mean.'

'No. There's more than that.'

'What?'

'You need to keep your eyes open, that's all.'

'You can't tell me that and not say what about.'

'You'll know when you see it.'

'You are an inscrutable fucking ghost or whatever the hell you are.'

Lonnie grinned and sipped his drink.

'How do you know I'm not an angel?'

I looked at him aghast.

'A ghoul I would believe. A demon from the seventh circle of hell, I would believe. An angel? Pull the other one, Lonnie.'

He snorted derisively.

'It's only because of my size. Everyone thinks angels are supposed to be tall and have expansive wings.'

'Well, aren't they?' I asked.

'Isn't Cupid a sort of angel? He's small.'

I shook my head in horror.

'If you start flying about the place, stark bollock naked,

firing a bow and arrow at people, I will personally buy a shotgun and shoot you down! For the good of the wider community! Cupid – for the love of Jehovah! You have a heart attack and start to develop delusions of grandeur about yourself.'

'Just watch the film,' Lonnie said, clearly annoyed but also not a little amused at my reaction. 'I wouldn't expect you to understand matters of such an ethereal nature.'

I fell asleep in front of the TV around one. He was gone when I awoke, cold and lonely in the darkness.

The girl danced as I played a jig on the mandolin: 'Out on the Ocean'. We were down at the beach, so it seemed appropriate. She hopped, skipped, jumped, pirouetted and finally did a rapid cartwheel, all the time giggling with sheer joy and exuberance.

'Again, again!' she called when the tune came to an end, and I played another, a reel this time, 'Drowsy Maggie'. She squealed and capered off across the wet sand, kicking her legs behind her. She reached the waterline and dipped in a toe, taking it out in time to the music and splashing a beat.

'We sing now,' she said when she was too tired to dance any more.

'What songs do you know?' I asked.

'I know every song,' she said.

'Every song?'

A nod.

'No one knows *every* song.'

'I do. I have music inside my heart.'

I thought that was a beautiful thing to say, and decided to give her the benefit of the doubt.

'All right then. I'm going to sing you this song, and you can join in.'

' 'Kay.'

I played the intro, a sort of slow waltz, and then began to sing

'*Well they say from this valley you are leaving; I will miss your bright eyes and sweet smile; For they say you have taken the sunshine; that had brightened my path for a while.*'

She didn't sing, just listened quietly.

'*So come and sit by my side if you love me; do not hasten to wish me adieu; but remember the Red River Valley; and the cowboy who loved you so true.*'

'Him goin' way?'

'No, I think she is.'

'Leavin' dere home?'

'Yes.'

'Me not never leavin' here.'

'Really?'

'Daddy says dis is our home. We can't never go 'way from it.'

'Oh. Well, if you like it I suppose that's good, isn't it?'

'Yeah.' She paused, gently plucking at the top string on the mandolin. 'Sometimes I think it'd be nice to go, though.'

'Well, when you're older you can go and do whatever you want.'

'No,' she said firmly. 'Daddy wouldn't like dat.'

'It'd be up to you,' I said.

'No, t'wouldn't,' she said. 'I has to stay. Fer ever and ever. Tha's de rules. And you don' wanna break de rules.'

8

I couldn't get Lonnie's words out of my head.

I was clearly aware that he was a figment of my imagination, some sort of strange mental episode brought on by grief, but I felt that this should not mean that he did not know what he was talking about. If my friend said something was not right, I was prepared to believe him.

Chaplin and I ate lunch the following day in a pub near the offices. Or rather I ate – he picked disconsolately at a chicken salad, taking up the individual pieces and nibbling on them before putting the frayed bits back down again. I had an open prawn sandwich on brown bread, and was not picking.

'You've been researching and writing about the Blaneys for years,' I said. 'What's the fascination? What makes them so compelling?'

'You were out there for nearly a day,' Chaplin retorted. 'Would you say they warrant further study?'

'From the point of view that they live in a veritable museum and live as if they were stuck in the Victorian era, yes, absolutely,' I said. 'But I reckon there's more to it than that.'

'This is still my story, Shane,' Chaplin said. 'I don't want you rooting about in it without my say so.'

'I am purely expressing idle interest,' I lied. 'But look, even if I did dig about, I would pass any and all information I unearthed on to you. Okay?'

'Fair enough. So what do you want to know?'

'Why have you made them your hobby?'

'The Blaneys *are* the history of this town. Pieter de Ponse de Blaney built the castellum that is the oldest part of the Blaney's house in 1344. In 1347 the Brothers of the Grey Cowl came here and built a monastery where the parish church is now. Over the next decade the town sprang up around it, with the Blaney family and their men as the protectors and rulers.'

'You're describing the way most towns developed during the medieval period,' I said. 'The religious orders were attracted to the big houses for protection, and the people came because they knew they could trade with the community of monks, and receive protection from the big house into the bargain.'

'Every major event that took place in this town – the fire that nearly destroyed it in 1463, the visit of Henry VII in 1501 – all these things were brought about by the Blaneys. As the years passed, the estate fell into ruin, and towards the end of the nineteenth century the family kind of separated into two wings. One side wanted to remain with the house and the land, try to rediscover their former greatness, the other wanted to sell up and use the capital to found a business empire. Tom represents the old school, his brother Gerry the new.'

'You indicated that Gerry is doing very well.'

'He is the richest man hereabouts. Tom may, in actual fact, be richer, he has so much stuff hidden away in the house, but Gerry is better off in terms of fluid, cash money. He owns a car showroom, a pub, a hotel, a waste recycling plant, a factory that makes fertilizer . . . I could go on. He has a finger in every pie in town, and he is not afraid to let anyone know it. He has the capacity to appear charming – something Tom

75

does not – but don't be fooled. Gerry is a snake in human form. He will crush you and think nothing of it.'

'Do Tom's kids go to school?'

'No. Dora is a qualified teacher – I think she taught in a primary school a couple of villages over, actually. Tom has them home-schooled by her.'

'So the kids never leave the estate?'

'You'll come across them in town occasionally, but it's a rarity.'

'They're pretty isolated then.'

'Very. But that's how Tom likes it. I mean, it's clear he *is* being terrorized, but he had begun to develop a siege mentality years ago all by himself. He thinks it's him against the rest of the world. This business with Gerry doesn't help.'

'Have you talked to Gerry about what's going on? Get his side of the story?'

'No.'

'Can I do it?'

Chaplin raised an eyebrow, but then smiled.

'You go ahead, son,' he said. 'I can't wait to hear what you make of him, not to mention what he makes of you.'

9

Gerry Blaney's car dealership was five miles outside of Garshaigh, on the Cork Road. I parked outside the showroom, and paused, peering through the glass front to see if I could make out the reason for my visit. The only person in evidence was a young woman with lots of blonde hair seated behind a high counter.

'Do you have an appointment, sir?' she asked in a lilting Southern accent – it could have been Cork or Tipperary, I wasn't sure.

'I don't,' I said, trying to look apologetic. 'Would you see if he could make some room in his schedule to see me?'

'He is very busy, Mr . . . uh . . .'

'Dunphy.'

'Mr Dunphy. But I'll ask him if he might be able to squeeze you in.'

I wandered about among the cars while she spoke on the phone. The place was, in essence, a glorified used car lot. Blaney didn't seem to specialize in one particular make or model – instead he filled the space with cars of various vintages and brands. I had to admit to myself that if I were in the market for a runabout, and needed it fast this was the sort of place I would gravitate to.

'Shane Dunphy,' a voice behind me said and, turning, I found myself face to face with a man in his late forties dressed in an expensive suit and smiling a smile that showed the attention of a lot of expensive dental work.

Gerry Blaney was tiny. Not as small as Lonnie, but not a lot bigger. I placed him at perhaps five foot one inch in height, and that last inch was mostly hair, which was died a creamy brown and piled high on his small head. He had spent time either in the tropics or on a sun bed recently, because he was dark walnut in complexion. His suit hung well on him, and he had a huge diamond pinkie ring. A thick gold bracelet hung from his skinny wrist. He was small and brash and vulgar. And despite all of that, charisma oozed from him.

'Gerry Blaney,' I smiled back, extending my hand, which he took and pumped vigorously.

'You've decided to grace our little burgh with your journalistic abilities,' he said. 'I've read some of your work in the nationals. I'm not going to pretend to agree with your politics, but I can admire the work of a professional when I see it. Welcome to Garshaigh.'

Trying not to appear as flattered by these words as I was (I had only ever met family members who could recall having read my work), I said something fluffy and non-committal and followed Gerry to his office.

'So how can I help you?' he asked, taking a bottle of expensive Scotch from a shelf at his ear and offering me a glass.

'I'm helping Robert Chaplin out with a story relating to a certain land dispute you seem to be involved in,' I said, taking the drink and sitting down on the chair Blaney indicated.

'Robert has always taken an unhealthy interest in my family's affairs,' Gerry said, though there was no anger in his voice. 'I often wondered if it was because he was an orphan himself – he kind of adopted the Blaneys.'

I had not known my boss was an orphan. It felt somehow intrusive to find out this way. I made a note to myself not to mention it to Chaplin.

'Your brother asked us to run the story,' I said. 'He claims you have gone to war with him over his inheritance. I witnessed him and his son being threatened by four men who were trying to get them to sell the house and land to the conglomerate who are developing the coastline.'

'And these men you saw said they were representing me?'

'No,' I admitted. 'But they certainly didn't deny it. Gerry, they threatened the children. Apparently Dora has been attacked in the past. This is a nasty business.'

Gerry sipped his whisky and looked at me. He had relaxed back into his seat and looked comfortable, relaxed. My line of questioning was certainly not upsetting him one iota.

'What do you want me to say, Shane? Am I contesting my father's will and Tom's right to be sitting on all that land and letting it rot with the weeds and the briars when it could be used to further the economic welfare of the entire community? Yes, I am. I have long suspected that my father was psychiatrically ill when he died, and that the will which was current, and was subsequently adhered to, was therefore null and void. I have spoken to the psychiatrist who treated my father, and he is in full agreement with me and has signed an affidavit to that effect. However, I am not sending armed henchmen to intimidate Tom, and I would never, ever, verbally or otherwise, bring harm on my nieces and nephews. I love those children as if they were my own.'

'So who do you think is trying to hurt them then?'

'I'd go and talk to the people out at Midden Industries. They're the ones looking to develop the land. Their current site of choice isn't winning them any friends. I expect they are anxious to find another.'

I nodded.

'That makes sense.'

Gerry smiled benignly.

'I have heard that you are a powerful man around Garshaigh,' I said.

'I have some influence,' Gerry said. He was the one who was flattered now.

'Seeing as your nieces and nephews are being openly threatened, do you feel motivated to do something about it?'

Gerry seemed to wince for a moment. It was only fleeting, though.

'I do and I shall,' he said. 'I'll find out who is behind all this, and put a stop to it. You see if I don't.'

I put my glass back on his table and stood.

'That's good,' I said. 'I thought they were really nice kids. I'd hate to think somebody was pushing them around.'

He gave me a sort of half wave and I left him deep in thought. When I got out to the car I rang Chaplin and told him about my visit.

'Seems like you got the upper hand,' my editor said. 'This time. Don't get cocky. You've just poked a crocodile with a stick – you might catch it napping the first time, but the second you're liable to lose an arm.'

'I hear you,' I said. 'Listen, while the details of the case are fresh in my mind, I'm going to head out to the Blaney house.'

'What in the hell for?'

'I'm just following a hunch. I'll call you later.'

I hung up while he was still spluttering down the line.

10

There was a strong wind blowing in from the sea when I got out to the house. I knocked as hard as I could, and rattled the rope inside the old ship's bell someone had hung outside one of the doors, but no one answered. I walked around the side and followed a narrow gravel path that ran about the outline of the structure. Every time I came across a window I knocked and hallooed, but only the crows answered, and it began to look as if I had wasted my time.

I walked back to the car, only to find a visitor sitting in the driver's seat.

'Hello, Emma,' I said.

The little girl was pretending to drive, trying to turn the wheel, reaching out for pedals with her feet.

'I was hoping to see your dad,' I said. 'Is he around?'

'I'm goin' in to town in this car,' Emma said. 'Wanna come?'

'Well,' I said. 'I do need to go back into town actually, I've got to see my boss before I go home, so a lift would be great, thanks.'

I opened the passenger side door and got in. Emma was still wearing the same shapeless dress, except it had one or two more stains on it than it had the last time I had seen her. Her blonde hair, still a mass of ringlets, had a greasy, unwashed quality and the child was still barefoot.

'So what are you going in to town for?' I asked.

'Shoppin',' the girl said.

'Shopping for what?'

'A new dress for my mammy and for Winnie and for me.'

'That all? Just clothes?'

'I'm gonna go into a café an' get me a lovely cream cake.'

'Yummy yummy!' I said.

Reaching over slowly (I remembered the startle reflex I had seen on my last visit), I opened the glove compartment and took out a bag of sweets I kept there for long car journeys. They were a mixture of all kinds – the type you scoop into the bag and them bring to the checkout to have weighed. The brown bag contained jelly babies, liquorice allsorts, chocolate mice and a myriad other varieties. I held it out so it was under my blonde companion's nose.

'Do you think some of these might keep you going until you get there?'

'Wow!' Emma crowed, grabbing the bag with both hands (I silently thanked the powers that be that we weren't really driving). 'Can I have some of them sweets?'

'You sure can,' I said.

I realized almost instantly that I had made a mistake, as the child began to cram fistfuls of the candy into her mouth completely indiscriminately. Usually when offered a sweet from such an eclectic selection, children can spend long minutes deciding which one to munch first. Not Emma – she had no such scruples.

'Hey, hey,' I said, putting my hand on the bag. 'You're going to make yourself sick!'

She stopped immediately, her big blue eyes on me, wondering

if I was now going to take the treat back as quickly as I had produced it.

'One at a time,' I said. 'If you eat all that sugar that fast, you'll just puke it all back up again.'

She slowed, stuffing only one or two at a time into her mouth in one go. I took a bottle of water from the cup holder and offered her some. She gulped some down.

'I think you are pretty hungry,' I said.

She nodded, turning back to the sweets. I wished I had brought a sandwich or some fruit. I hated seeing her gorge on such rubbish, but I didn't have anything else to offer her.

'Did you miss breakfast or something?'

'Some days we don't have breakfuss,' she said.

'What about lunch?'

'We had lunch when you was here, 'member?'

'And you haven't had lunch since then?'

Emma shook her head. I felt anger starting to prickle about the base of my neck.

'Where's your mum and dad?' I asked. 'Or even Jim or Winnie? You aren't here all by yourself, are you?'

'I don't know where they are,' she said. 'What does that button do?'

She was pointing at the radio on the dashboard of the Austin.

'That switches on the radio. Your dad has a jeep. It must have a radio.'

She shook her head.

I turned the switch and the radio lit up. I fiddled with it until I found a music station. Paul McCartney was singing 'Ob-La-Di Ob-La-Da', from *The White Album*.

'This is brilliant,' I said. 'Come on!'

I jumped out, leaving the door open, and opened her door too, scooping the child up in my arms.

'When you have music like this, you have to dance,' I said, and started singing and dancing along to the wonderful, silly song, skipping from foot to foot on the gravel and earth of the Blaney's front yard. Emma giggled uncontrollably, clearly having the time of her life. Sir Paul and I sang about Desmond and Molly, their barrow in the marketplace, the band, Desmond's proposal, their new home and their grow-ing family, all punctuated by the infectious, nonsense chorus. The child learned the words to it quickly, and joined in with great gusto.

'More, more!' she begged when it was over.

'You have to let me get my breath back for a second,' I said. 'Or maybe you can carry me for the next one.'

The next song was Creedence Clearwater Revival's 'Bad Moon Rising', which required more athletic boogying. I was in the middle of the first chorus when the Blaney parents pulled up in their aforementioned jeep. I waved, as did Emma. Tom, on the other hand, had a face like thunder, and the door open before his vehicle had even stopped.

'What in the hell are you doin' here?'

'I came to see you, as it happens. When I couldn't get an answer I thought you might be in another part of the house, which, of course, you weren't, and when I got back to my car, this little one was sitting in the driver's seat. You really shouldn't leave her unattended, you know.'

'Winnie was meant to be minding her!'

'Winnie isn't here,' I said calmly.

'And what is that god-awful music?'

'That's Creedence,' I said. 'I like it.'

'I like it too,' Emma said, which made him even more annoyed.

'I have gone to great lengths to ensure that my children are not exposed to the dross that is pumped out by the media.

And now you come along with your fancy car and your hi-tech radio and your modern music '

I couldn't but intercede at this juncture.

'Hold on there just one cotton pickin' moment!' I said. 'My *fancy car* is a vintage model, way older than your jeep. The radio is an original push button, hardly hi-tech, and the song you refer to as "modern music" dates back to 1969! I'm hardly bombarding the girl with the twenty-first century now, am I?'

Tom stuttered and stammered for a moment, clearly a bit blindsided by these facts. I put Emma down and tousled her hair.

'I came out to tell you I'd been chatting to your brother, and I think I may have shamed him in to calling off his goons. But you seem to have things under control here.'

I walked back to the Austin and then turned back to Tom.

'I got the impression your daughter there is hungry, that she might have missed some meals. Now, seeing as how you have more money than Santa Claus and the Count of Monte Cristo put together, I'm sure that has to be a mistake or an oversight.' I waved at Emma and smiled when she waved back.

'Bye bye sweetie. I enjoyed our dance very much.'

'B'bye,' she said.

I drove away cursing myself. I was worried I might have done more harm than good. But then, I was quite used to that.

11

The class listened closely. I had turned all the lights off except that which was thrown by the PowerPoint projector. On the board at the top of the room was the flickering image of a handsome, athletic-looking man in fatigues, carrying a camera. Gathered about him was a group of what looked like children but were, on closer examination, clearly adults of very small stature.

'The Mbuti pygmy are one of the oldest indigenous populations in the world,' I said. 'They live in the Ituri forest, a tropical jungle covering about 70,000 square kilometres in the northeast of the Democratic Republic of the Congo, in what we used to call Zaire. The Mbuti have been about since at least the year 2500 BC, when they were mentioned on an Egyptian stone tablet. Their lifestyle hasn't changed much since then – they remain one of the few true hunter-gatherer groups in the world, and they still live in incredibly isolated communities deep in one of the most inhospitable jungles imaginable.'

I looked about me. All faces were attentive, rapt in concentration.

'Despite all this, they are one of the most studied of all native peoples. Since that first Egyptian explorer came across them, the Mbuti have proven to be a very friendly, welcoming group. They warmly include outsiders into their homes and will happily talk about their lives and their ways. Sociologists have been spending time with them for almost a hundred years, now. I want you to imagine that you are a documentary maker, and have been asked to produce a programme on the Mbuti. The only way you can get to their village is by helicopter, after which you have to hike for several hours to get to the settlement proper. When that whirlybird takes off, you know you are all alone with the tribe until it comes back – probably in two months' time. Until then, you have to fend for yourself as best you can.'

I stood and clicked the mouse to bring up another slide.

'What do you think would be the main things you'd have trouble with,' I asked. 'In which areas would you struggle?'

I looked about the room and there, with her hand held aloft, was Gladys. Pleased, I nodded in her direction.

'What do you reckon would be your greatest challenge, Gladys?' I asked.

'The biggest problem any of us is gonna have is that them little fellas ain't real.'

I shook my head. I wasn't following.

'Who's not real?'

'Them little lads. They don't really exist.' This last statement said in a loud whisper, as if trying to break it to me gently.

'Gladys, I assure you, there *is* such a thing as pygmies. They are very real. There are about 40,000 of them in the Ituri rainforest alone, so in the grander scheme of things they are quite successful.'

Gladys was shaking her head sadly, as if I had completely lost my mind.

'He'll be telling us leprechauns is real next,' she said to the person next to her. 'He must think we're awfully thick.'

*　*　*

I had to run home at the break and get a book to prove to Gladys (and a few of the others who were beginning to believe her, so convincing were her protestations) that the Mbuti were a real people and not just a figment of my or anyone else's imagination.

'Jaysis,' she said, poring over the photos in the book. 'What next, eh? Is Bigfoot real too?'

Yet again, she had me stumped.

As I had not had time for a cup of coffee at the break, I left the class leafing through the book I had brought, and hurried up to grab a cup. As I spooned coffee into a cafetière, I heard steps behind me, and Carla, the pretty waitress from the café, came in.

'Everything okay?' I asked.

'Um . . . no, actually,' she said. 'I wasn't sure who I should talk to about this.'

'Well, I'm here,' I said. 'Sit down. If I can help you, I will.'

Carla was as tall as me, slim, with thick dark hair and a fresh friendly face. She dressed in a hippyish style which I had noticed the younger people about Garshaigh tended to favour.

'This is really embarrassing,' she said, and passed her mobile phone over to me.

'What do you want me to do with this?' I asked, picking it up.

'Read the message that's on the screen.'

I touched the screen and it lit up. There was a short message there, and I did as she asked. It was the sort of message one person sends to another when they are in a very intimate relationship, and that person desires to get intimate again very soon. It made me blush.

'Carla . . . I'm not sure why . . .'

'That isn't from my boyfriend,' she said.

I looked up at her.

'There are twenty others like it on my phone, all sent within the past two weeks. All from the same number.'

'Have you or your boyfriend rung the number?'

'No one ever answers.'

'I think the thing to do would be to go to the police,' I said. 'You can get the number blocked. And they can probably have the owner traced.'

Carla laughed, cynically.

'I know who's doing it,' she said.

'You do?'

'Oh yeah.'

'Who is it?'

'That fucking *asshole* Jeff McKinney.'

'The guy in the wheelchair?'

'The very one.'

'How'd he get your number?'

Carla laughed again.

'I *gave* it to him. Sure he was always coming in and out of the café always alone. I felt sorry for the fucker. He started talking to me one day about some issue he said they were having with the service system in the hotel, and I gave him some advice, and before I knew it, he was asking for my number so he could call to clarify – and I didn't think, I just wrote it on a napkin and gave it to him.'

'Have you tried talking to him?'

'No. I'd kill him if I did.'

'What about your boyfriend?'

'He doesn't want to – he says if we ignore the problem, it'll go away.'

'I'm not sure about that,' I said. 'He looks quite committed to the whole thing just now.'

'It creeps me out,' Carla said. 'I feel like he's been going through my things. I mean, I know he *hasn't* but that's how it feels.'

'Do you want *me* to talk to him? I'd be happy to.'

She shook her head and patted the back of my hand.

'No. I think I just needed to let off steam. To vent.'

'Are you sure?'

'Yes, yes really. Get your coffee. Let's do some learning.'

I pushed the plunger and poured myself a cup.

'Let's do that,' I said.

After class Gladys was at my desk again.

'I'm sorry I gave ya a hard time there, Shane.'

'That's okay,' I said. 'I did say I wanted you to speak up if something was on your mind. I don't mind being challenged. It shows you're thinking.'

'So why do I feel like an idiot then?'

'I hope I didn't make you feel that way,' I said.

'No. It's just . . . I'm not a big reader, see? I haven't looked at a book since I left school, and I don't really watch the documentary channels a whole lot either. So stuff like you was talkin' about, tribes and stuff – I don't know about that.'

'The class wasn't really about the Mbuti,' I said. 'I used them as an example to get everyone thinking about the process of socialization – how we learn to behave within the communities where we live. I don't expect anyone to walk out of here this evening thinking that they've spent the whole night being taught about pygmy lifestyle.'

'Is there any books I can read?' Gladys asked.

'About what?' I asked. 'I can recommend loads of books, but they might not be about what you want.'

'I don't know – you were reading a book last time during the break. What was that about?'

I took the book from the shelf below my desk.

'This is called *Dibs* and it's about a little boy going to see a play therapist. It's sort of a classic in the field of childcare. You can borrow it if you like.'

Dibs is not a thick book, which is attractive if you're a little bit afraid of reading. Gladys picked it up and turned it over in her hand, as if to read the blurb on the back.

'Is it easy to read?'

'Yeah. The author, a woman called Virginia Axline, gets a bit flowery at times, but in the main it's easy enough. It should only take a few sittings to get it finished.'

Gladys looked nervously at the print, which was quite small.

'I don't know. I'm not good with books.'

'You asked me, Gladys,' I said. 'I'm not trying to force it on you. And there is no onus on you to take it anyway. I won't think any less of you if you decide to give it a miss.'

The woman chewed her lower lip, flicked through the pages as if speed-reading them, then in a surge of movement tossed the book back at me and darted away from the desk and out the door of the room. I sat where I was, convinced that I must have done something to bring on that kind of behaviour. When I couldn't work out what it was, I got up and went home.

The girl looked at me with a strange expression.

'Wha' you talkin' bout?'

'Okay, let's start again,' I said. 'You just asked me a question about butterflies. I don't know the answer.'

'You don' know?'

'No, I don't. But, see, what I *can* do is, when I go home, I can switch on my computer and ask *it* the question, and it will find out the answer for me.'

'What a compoother?'

'It's a machine that is linked up to millions and millions of people all over the world, and it can look in lots and lots of different books and files until it finds the answer to your question, and then it brings it back to me. And it does all this in about three seconds.'

'How?'

'It's really, really fast.'

'You see it runnin' 'round?'

'No. The answer is sent down the telephone wires – sort of . . .'

'So it's really, really small?'

'Um . . . no . . . it's like as big as a book. Maybe a little bigger.'

'How it fit in the wire then?'

'No, you plug the wire into it.'

'It have books inside it?'

'In a way, yes.'
'Why not jus' look for de answer in a book den?'
I had to admit, she had a point.

12

It was seven o'clock in the evening and I had put in a long day at the newspaper offices. I had written yards of column inches on topics as diverse as local government elections, potholes, a dog show in the community centre, the price of heating oil, potholes, another meeting of the anti-development protesters, a lady in Garshaigh who was having her ninety-ninth birthday, and potholes. I was locking up the door to the street when I felt a tap on the shoulder and turned to find two of the men who had tried (and failed) to intimidate Tom Blaney.

'Hello,' I said, feeling a sinking feeling in the pit of my stomach. I suspected that I would be a much easier target.

'You're to stay away from the Blaney place,' the man whom Jim Blaney had punched said.

Now I was confused. I was so befuddled, the feeling totally cancelled out any sense of fear or dread.

'Why?' I asked in genuine bafflement.

'Just do as you're told unless you want a beatin',' the other goon, the squat, fat one, said. He pronounced the word 'beatin'' to sound like 'baitin''.

'Look, you can give me the hiding of my life, but if my boss directs me to go out there, then I'll have to go. And it just doesn't make any sense – I mean, if you told me to stop bugging *Gerry* Blaney, well, I could see how that would work. But to warn me away from the guy I *saw you* attempting to scare . . . boys, you've got me at a loss.'

The two glanced at each other and decided to cut their losses.

'Don't say we didn't warn ye,' the first guy said, grabbing me by the scuff of the neck and giving me a half-hearted shake.

'All right, all right,' I said as they headed off into the early evening. 'You two have a good night.'

I walked home shaking my head. The Blaney situation was getting stranger by the day.

13

The warning made me want to drive out to the Blaney homestead immediately, but I managed to hold off until the following morning. This time I brought some sandwiches, fruit, biscuits and cartons of juice. Just in case.

It was one of those beautiful early autumn days when Ireland seems to be the best place in the world to be. The wild, rugged landscape about the Blaneys' wild, rugged house was a deep gold in colour, the stubbled corn and untended reeds and grass grey and dark green against the sandy brown of the dried earth. Plovers nested amid the clumps and a kestrel hovered above, waiting for something to put a foot wrong.

Tom was not happy to see me this time either.

'How many different ways do I need to tell you to leave us alone?' he asked, barring the door with his big frame.

'What's the matter Tom?' I asked. 'Don't you love me anymore? I would have thought that we would have had some kind of bond after what we've been through together. A band of brothers, isn't that what they call it?'

'You're off your fuckin' head,' he snarled.

'I was paid a visit last night by some of the goons you and Jim ran into before,' I said. 'They told me to keep away from you and your family. That sounds a lot like what you've just said to me. They working for you now?'

Tom blinked and suddenly looked deeply confused.

'No – Jesus, no, of course not. You'd better come in after all.'

He brought me to the living area and we sat in more or less the same places we had last time.

'I'm sorry you had to get mixed up in all this,' he said. 'I can look after me own, but I wouldn't want you gettin' hurt.'

I waved it off.

'I don't think they seriously meant to harm me,' I said. 'It's a big deal to meddle with a journalist after that reporter Veronica Guerin's murder. They don't look like nice people, but they don't look terribly professional either, do they? I mean, they must have known you'd have a gun and not be afraid to use it, but still they came with just . . . well, with big sticks.'

'So what are you going to do?'

'Nothing. Continue to help Chaplin cover the story of the trial. Call out the odd time to see how things are going from your end. I don't see there's much else I can do.'

He nodded and hugged his knees, an odd gesture for a man so large. He suddenly seemed to be a big child.

'My Emma is rightly taken with you. She said you were right nice to her.'

'She's a nice kid. It's not hard to take to her.'

As if on cue, a knocking was heard from above us, and looking up at one of the small windows that had been set at irregular intervals about the top of the room, I saw Emma's pixie-like face grinning down at me.

'Do I want to know how she got up there?' I asked.

'Probably not,' Tom said truthfully.

* * *

97

I went outside to find Emma and her older brother, Dom, sitting on the narrow ledge of the window. I reached up and lifted them both down, setting them on the ground in front of me.

'You could have fallen and hurt yourselves,' I said. 'Maybe you could try and be a little bit more careful?'

'He gave me sweets,' Emma said conspiratorially to her sibling.

I couldn't suppress a smile.

'Oh, so you remember the sweets, do you?'

Emma nodded. Dom eyed me cautiously.

'I'll tell you what,' I said. 'You take me for a walk down to the beach and I'll give you something nice that I have in my bag here. We can have a bit of a picnic. What do you say?'

There was no need for any discussion. The pair grabbed one of my hands each and we headed off at a canter across the field next to the house.

Emma was a real chatterbox, while Dom, still a little unsure of me and my motives, was far more restrained. The girl wanted to sing the two songs we had learned on 'that fancy damned radio thing'. So I sang the chorus of 'Ob-La-Di' again, and at first just Emma, but soon both kids, joined in merrily. Once we'd sang that a few times we tried 'Bad Moon Rising', and that was just as successful.

'Can I listen to songs on your radio, mister?' Dom asked as we walked.

'Your dad wasn't very happy about it,' I said.

'No, he weren't,' Emma said gravely.

'So I don't know if I can really do something your father wouldn't approve of,' I said.

'I don't know why he hates so much stuff,' Dom said sulkily. 'We're never let do nuthin'. What's wrong with just hearin' a few songs, eh? It won't hurt nobody.'

'You'll get in bad trouble again,' Emma said, looking ominously at her brother. 'You don't want to get beat on again, do you? 'Cause that's what'll happen.'

I was bursting to intercede at this point, to question just exactly what 'getting beat on' might mean, but I held back. *That is not why you're here! Get them talking about these threats, not about their domestic problems!*

We got to the beach and I found myself very close to the place where I had taken my dip that first day in Garshaigh.

'This is our beach,' Emma said. 'Nobody ever comes here. It's just for us, so it is.'

We sat and I laid out the food, using my jacket as a table cloth. I had erred on the side of caution with the sandwiches, going for plain ham. The apples were Pink Ladies, crisp and sweet, and I'd brought a mix of biscuits – plain, chocolate, oatmeal, creams and marshmallows. I was not even slightly surprised when the whole lot disappeared rapidly.

'That was lovely!' Emma said, lying back on the sand.

'I'm stuffed,' Dom agreed. 'Thanks, mister.'

'Would you please call me Shane,' I asked, playfully poking him in the ribs. At the barest touch, the boy cringed.

'Hey,' I said, 'I'm sorry. Did I hurt you, Dom?'

'No. I'm fine,' he said, though he clearly wasn't.

'Why don't we play a game?' I suggested, wanting to take the focus off Dom.

'What kind of a game?' Emma asked, sitting up, excited already.

'Well, we're on the beach,' I said. 'How about we make the biggest sandcastle we can manage?'

'But we don't gots no buckets or shovels or nothin'!' Dom said, obviously still a bit off colour.

'Follow me, my young friends,' I said.

Within seconds we had found three flat pieces of wood

that more than adequately acted as spades, not to mention two plastic pots, one an old margarine container, the other an empty travel mug, which would do very nicely as buckets.

'Right,' I said. 'Let's see if we can't construct the most amazing, fantabulous, coolest sandcastle that was ever built, on this or any other beach!'

'Yeah!'

'For sure!'

We worked hard on that castle for the next hour, and I can report that it was impressive. I would have had great fun had I not noticed, five minutes after we started, the deep, black bruises that could be seen whenever Dom's T-shirt rode up as he bent or stretched to pat down some sand or to dig the moat. These were not bruises that a boy of twelve would come across in the normal rough and tumble of his life. Someone had beaten Dom badly, about the body, where his clothes would hide it.

I just wasn't sure who.

But I could hazard a guess.

14

I caught Robert Chaplin just before he went home for the evening.

'Where you been?'

'Out at the Blaneys. Thought I'd tell Tom about the warning I received.'

'I've called the boys in blue about that,' Chaplin said. 'They're going to be watching the offices as we come and go for a bit.'

'Good. Listen, Robert, there's something I want to run by you, and I want you to think about it before you blow a gasket.'

Looking as if his gaskets were lining up ready for imminent explosion, Chaplin sat back behind his desk.

'You will agree with me that the Blaney way of life is a little on the strange side. Not exactly conducive to comfort or even exemplary personal hygiene.'

'Yes,' Chaplin said, waiting for the hammer to fall.

'It would be difficult to ignore the fact that the children are all fairly manky, their clothes are ill-fitting and unwashed, and they seem to be very small for their ages.'

Chaplin narrowed his eyes as if he were trying to work out my next step.

'I'll grant you're right about all those points, yes,' he said. 'But I bet you've seen similar things in the children of hippies and new agers. It's not a crime to be a bit mucky.'

'Mmm. But I don't think Emma even owns a pair of shoes,' I said. 'I've certainly never seen her wear any.'

'Means nothing,' Chaplin said. 'My own daughter wouldn't wear anything other than a pair of shorts and some pink Wellington boots for three months when she was two. Had her poor mother driven to distraction.'

'I was out there two days ago and Emma told me that she hadn't had lunch since the first day we went out. She was half-starved. She nearly took the hand and all off me when I offered her something to eat.'

'What'd you give her?'

'I had some sweets in the car '

'Sweets? She took the hand off you when you offered her some sweets? Shane, I don't doubt for one single second that those children are starved of sweets and popcorn and I am certain they have never been to the cinema and are never going to see the hallowed halls of Walt Disney World. I'll bet she grabbed those sweets and tried to horse them down her before her parents arrived. God knows when she'll see something sugary again.'

'It's more than that,' I said, feeling like I was being made fun of. 'Those kids are genuinely hungry!'

'Really? How do you reckon?'

'I brought sandwiches and biscuits and some fruit out today.'

'You brought mass-produced bread slathered in butter and chocolate biscuits. Yet again, what do you expect the children to do? They'll be on a sugar high for a week.'

'Dom has bruises, Robert. I saw them myself. And Emma talked about him being beaten.'

Chaplin sighed and tutted, rattling his pen off the desk top.

'I might not like Tom Blaney. He is a nasty piece of work, and I believe that whatever is going on over this land sale is crooked as a pretzel. But I do not believe he is in any way neglecting or physically abusing his children. He dotes on those kids. What you're describing can be explained in half a dozen totally plausible ways.'

'I'm not sure I agree with you, Robert,' I said. 'I used to do this kind of work, and I know neglect when I see it. I also know, without any doubt, that Dom was beaten. It may not have been Tom. Remember, those gorillas were threatening the children, too.'

Chaplin considered that.

'I don't like it,' he said. 'But it's possible. I'll put it to Tom the next time I'm out there.'

'Thanks, Robert,' I said. 'One final question.'

'Shoot.'

'You told me that the kids were all home schooled.'

'Yeah.'

'All of them?'

Chaplin paused, chewing his lower lip and thinking.

'If I remember correctly, Jim, the eldest boy, went to primary school for a bit locally, but they took him out before he made his confirmation.'

'That's great. Let's get out of here before those cops get bored waiting for us.'

'And before you start to suspect Mrs Chaplin is mistreating me.'

'Well who could blame her,' I said, and we left the office laughing.

As I said goodbye to Chaplin, I noticed Jeff McKinney parked across the road, watching us. I made to cross over to speak to him, but he rolled off at a tremendous speed before I got through the home-time traffic.

15

I rang George Taylor and asked him if he happened to know the principal of the local primary school.

'I used to work there,' he informed me.

'Could you effect an introduction?'

'Do you propose to do some teaching there also?'

'No. This is purely an act of pastoral care.'

'Oh.'

'When you let your colleague know I will be calling, could you stress my previous child protection credentials?'

'I will certainly mention them. Shane, is this something I need to be concerned about?'

'I don't think so. Thanks for your help, Mr Taylor.'

'Well. All right. I shall see you tomorrow night then.'

'I'll be there.'

The principal of Garshaigh National School was a woman named Nathalie Lassiter. She was about forty-five with brunette hair and was dressed in a dark purple trouser suit. She shook my hand and offered me coffee from a tray on her desk.

'George tells me you are a former child protection worker,' she said when we were seated.

'He lets you call him George?'

'No. I just do it behind his back,' she said with a grin.

'I feel less marginalized with that knowledge,' I said.

'How can I help you, Shane?'

'I want to begin by asking that whatever is said in this office remains here.'

'I have no problem with confidentiality under the correct circumstances. I believe that – as well as teaching on George's night school, you also work for the local newspaper . . .'

'Everything that passes between us here is off the record,' I said. 'What I want to talk to you about came to my attention through a story I was researching, but will not be included as part of it.'

'And should it become pertinent to any legal proceedings?' Nathalie asked tentatively.

'Your name will never be mentioned,' I assured her. 'This meeting never happened.'

'All right,' she said, 'proceed. I do not promise that I will give you any information, but if I think it appropriate for me to do so, I will help you.'

'Thank you,' I said. 'That's as much as I would have expected. I want to ask you about Jim Blaney.'

Nathalie nodded and added some hot coffee to my mug, then hers.

'It has been three years – maybe a little more – since he left the school, and I have been waiting for someone to come asking about him,' she said. 'I never thought it would be a journalist.'

'I'm not here in that capacity. Did you have any concerns about him?'

Nathalie shrugged. 'What do you mean by the term "concerns"?'

'Well, as a primary school teacher, what would be the kinds

of things that would normally make you worry about a student's welfare?'

'Behavioural difficulties; sexualized behaviour; clear signs of neglect like repeated failure to bring in lunch, the lack of appropriate clothing for the weather; the continuous appearance of injuries that cannot be explained – are these the things you mean?'

'Well they're a good start,' I said. 'I'm aware that every child is different and will elicit different concerns – but did any of those issues arise with Jim Blaney?'

'Almost all of them. He was a concern from the very first day he arrived here. He had difficulty mixing with the other children and was constantly in fights; he reeked of ammonia and body odour; he never had a lunch with him and stole food from the other children. Of course he was automatically singled out because the family had no television. You'd be amazed at how many conversations are made up of discussions of TV shows and computer games. The poor boy would try and pretend he had seen the shows or played the games, but of course he had absolutely no idea what they were talking about and was found out rapidly. He responded to these moments of embarrassment with violence.'

'Did you try to talk to his parents?'

'I sent notes home. They were ignored. I couldn't ring them, obviously, as they have no telephone. I waited with bated breath for the parent teacher meeting, but predictably they did not turn up for it.'

'So what did you do?'

'We had our own meeting here at the school and decided the best thing to do was to make sure he had food when he was here, that he had clean clothes (sitting next to him could be very uncomfortable for the other child), and we tried to teach him as best we could.'

'How'd that go?'

'I flatter myself into thinking it went very well. The lady who taught him in junior infants took him aside and told him that there would be a packed lunch waiting for him in the storage area every day, with a snack for the eleven o'clock break. Jim said not a word, but the following day he went to look, and it was there, and do you know, when he had some food inside him he was a different child. I'm not saying he didn't still get into fights, but it was less frequent and less vicious when it did happen.'

'So food made a huge difference.'

'Such a small thing.'

'How long was he at the school?'

'Right up until sixth class. He left just before Christmas.'

'What happened?'

'The children were doing Physical Education. Most of the kids brought in sports gear to change into – of course Jim never had any, and so participated in whatever clothes he had on. The PE teacher felt this was wrong, and found some he thought would fit. We did the usual foostering about to make it look like these were actually Jim's and not from goodwill. The kid was over the moon, couldn't wait for the PE class to roll around. Finally it did, and out the kids went to the gym. There's a locker room they change in, and generally we just leave them to it. But this particular day the teacher heard something of a ruckus – nothing extreme, but just a change in the general tone of the usual chatter.'

'They got louder?'

'No, he said they actually got quieter. When he went down he saw that Jim had taken off his T-shirt, to change into the sports top. He was, God love him, carefully folding his own ragged shirt. But what was causing the consternation among the rest of the group was his torso. It was covered in a patch-work pattern of bruises, scratches and cuts. That boy had been thrashed within an inch of his life.'

'And you went straight out to the Blaney homestead.'

'I drove Jim home. I never saw his father, but his mother sat and listened as I voiced the litany of issues we had, ending with the bruising. During the whole thing she looked as if I was battering her about the head. When I was finished she said she would discuss it with her husband, and showed me the door. I informed her that I would be passing my concerns on to the police, and she closed the door in my face.'

'And you never saw Jim again.'

'No. I knew he had siblings, and they never came to us – I'm told they were all home schooled – but for some reason Jim had been permitted to attend class. Not from then on. I did tell the police as I had promised, but I didn't hear any more about it.'

'Is it possible Jim received those bruises through rough play with his brothers and sisters?'

'No. There is no doubt in my mind the marks I saw were the result of a deliberate attempt by an adult to harm the child.'

'Did Jim ever give any indication as to who had marked him?'

'All he would say was that he had been a bad boy and needed to be punished. "I gotta put things right," he kept saying. I don't know how beating him to a pulp could achieve that.'

'Probably doesn't help to try and make sense of it,' I said.

'So what are you going to do now I've told you this grubby little story?' Nathalie asked.

'Damned if I know,' I said. 'It looks very much like those children are at risk out on the Blaney farm. What you've told me matches up with some stuff I've seen myself. What the authorities will do with it, I can't tell.'

'Didn't you used to be one of those authorities?'

'I'm not sure I was much of an authority on anything,' I said.

And I meant it.

16

I needed something to lighten my mood, so that evening I packed up my guitar, my ukulele and my autoharp, along with my djembe drum and some other percussion instruments, and brought them with me to class. I figured it was time to put the students through their paces.

That evening we spent the first hour looking at some of the guidelines around space, staffing ratios, sleeping arrangements, changing stations and other essential, though fairly dry and droll, matters in early years services. By the time tea break came around I knew they were all badly in need of a caffeine boost. I rapidly moved the chairs into a circle and got my instruments from the car. When everyone returned, I was sitting, facing the door, with my guitar slung across my lap, the autoharp on a stand beside me, the uke hanging from a table and the percussion equipment spread about the floor at my feet.

'Sit down for a moment,' I said ominously. 'I hope you all brought your voices.'

I could sense the worry emanating from some of them. This wasn't what they signed up for; they expected to spend their evenings discussing theories of child development, learning about the proper way to lay out a play area or supervise groups on outings. Now here I was moving the goalposts. I may have mentioned in passing that I sometimes brought in instruments, but not a person among them thought I would actually *do* it.

'The first thing I want is for everyone to relax,' I said, although most of the students still looked deeply unhappy. 'No one is going to have to sing on their own tonight unless they want to, and I'm going to ease you in to this type of activity very gently. I want you to think about this: you are all here to explore the idea of working with kids – whether or not you plan to do it full time, as occasional babysitters or childminders, or even as parents yourselves, a major part of that experience is using what we call 'creative play' – music, role play, art – and that involves making yourself a little bit vulnerable: giving something of yourselves. If you are going to ask the kids to do it, you have to be prepared to do it yourselves, too.'

'I don't mind making an idiot of myself in front of a bunch of two-year-olds,' Breda, a woman in her early fifties, piped up. 'It's different in a situation like this, though.'

'Why?' I asked mildly. 'Everyone will be in the same boat. I'm not asking you to do anything any childcare worker wouldn't be expected to do in an average day's work.'

The expressions that met mine were still distrustful and strained.

'Okay,' I said. 'The best way to get into this is to just . . . *get into it*. You see before you on the floor a djembe drum – basically a traditional African bongo. You can also probably identify a tambourine, a triangle, some toy cymbals and a maraca – a shaker. Who would like to have a go on any of those?'

No one moved.

'Come on,' I urged. 'I know someone out there is just dying to get at the djembe drum.'

Jessie, a beautiful, dark-haired, brown-eyed girl of about twenty-five shyly raised her hand. She had a sort of gypsy look about her, so I wasn't one bit surprised.

'Well done Jess,' I said, laughing. 'Take the drum.'

She did, tiptoeing over and scooping it up. Djembe drums come in all sizes, some tiny, others as large as your average dustbin. Mine is big enough to hold between your knees. I knew Jessie would enjoy it.

As soon as the drum had been claimed, the other percussion instruments were picked off quickly. It was as if the flood gates had been opened.

'Before we go any farther,' I said, 'does anyone in the group actually play something? For instance, if there are any guitarists among you, I can just switch over to the uke or the autoharp. I don't mind loaning you my strings one little bit.'

'I play the tin whistle – or at least I used to, in school,' said Maggie, a blonde woman in her thirties.

'The whistle is a beautiful instrument,' I agreed. 'I regret never having kept it up myself when I left school. Do you own one, Mag?'

She shook her head.

'Y'know, if you feel you'd like to take it up again, you'll buy a decent whistle for a few euro. Think about it.'

She nodded. Biddy, a girl with her hair dyed a bright red, had her hand up.

'I have an accordion at home.'

'Oh, I do love the accordion,' I said. 'Is it button or piano?'

She shook her head, confused.

'Does it have buttons, like the autoharp over there, or keys, like a piano?'

'Both,' she said.

'Then it's a piano accordion,' I said. 'Do you play it often?'

'I haven't played it in about five years. But I used to, though, a lot.'

'Well, I know I – and I'm sure the rest of the group will concur – would love you to bring it in here one evening to play for us. Will you think about that?'

Blushing deeply, Biddy nodded.

'Music is one of my favourite ways of getting a group to bond,' I said. 'Humans sang before they could speak. I've brought in percussion instruments for you all because drums were the very first instruments people made, back when they lived in caves and had to hunt to survive. Rhythm, the drum beat, speaks to us in a primal voice that we can hear right down deep in our souls. You know when you hear a song or a tune and you just can't help moving?'

Almost everyone nodded.

'That's the voice I'm talking about. Children can hear the truth in a song or a piece of music way, way better than they can hear most other things. I want to do a little experiment with you all this evening. We're going to get a rhythm going, with the instruments and with our hands and maybe even using some of the furniture, and we're going to build a song around it.'

I could see them beginning to settle in to the idea. I wasn't looking for them to get up and dance solo in front of everyone. No one was being made to perform, *X Factor* like, to be judged or ridiculed. In a way, this was just as much a discussion or academic exercise as anything else we'd done.

'The song we're going to use is one you all know, but probably don't know you know,' I said. 'It is what we call an *archetype*, which means it is the frame upon which hundreds of other songs are hung. It's called 'Train Coming Round the Bend', not a very exciting title, or even a very musical one, but when you hear it, you'll see that people like Johnny Cash, Elvis Presley, Jim Morrison and loads of others have used it to build their own songs on. 'Folsom Prison Blues' is probably the most famous, but as we sing, you'll find that lots of others will come to you, even some Irish ones. Now, here's the rhythm I want you to strike up and keep going. Just those with the rhythm instruments first, then we'll get the rest of you sorted.'

I beat a pattern on the body of my guitar.

'Jessie, try and copy that on the drum.'

She managed a pretty good facsimile.

'Now, Rachel, you fall in on the tambourine. Jess, keep going – we're trying to get a groove going here.'

I had to borrow the tambourine from Rachel to show her, but once she'd picked it up her beat was solid and steady. Within about ten minutes we had everyone in the room doing something, and I was amazed at how tight the tempo was.

'So now we lay down the vocal track,' I said.

Going over to my laptop I hit a key, and on the board the lyrics for the song appeared:

The train's coming around the bend
Goodbye my love, goodbye.
The train's coming around the bend
As the sun takes to the sky.

Farewell my dear today, I wish that I could stay
Please do not cry, goodbye my lover goodbye.

I fell into a driving rhythm on the guitar, and as soon as I did I sensed everyone in the room feeling the power of it. The identity of the author of the song has long been lost: it probably dates back to the workers on the first railroads in the US, and tells of the transient lives of these men, forced to leave home and family behind as they followed the iron horses across the continent. The melody is as simple as the lyric, a blues holler easily learned and incredibly satisfying to sing. I bellowed it out, waited a few beats and then repeated it. All about were smiling now. Some were clapping, others slapping tables, one or two were lifting chairs and then banging them to the ground on the beat, I even had a group using white-board markers as drum sticks against the wall.

'Your turn,' I said. 'I'll get you started, but I want to hear you all sing.'

They didn't need a second invitation. If I hadn't known better, I would have thought each and every one of them had lived the life of the migrant rail worker.

'Beautiful. Now, keep it going.'

I moved about the room, encouraging first one group then another. Jessie had gotten creative on the djembe and was trying rolls and fills with increasing confidence. Rachel was as steady as ever on the tambourine. My chair beaters had worked out a kind of alternating beat that was hilarious to see, but strangely effective. I was kind of swaying in time to their ministrations, singing a harmony line to the lead melody, when the door was flung open and a horrified-looking George Taylor stormed in. To the credit of the group, no one stopped playing.

'Hey Mr Taylor,' I said over the music. 'We're kind of in the middle of something here.'

'You can be heard on the street!' he said. 'And I don't think that whiteboard markers are meant to be used that way.'

'I'll replace any that are damaged,' I promised.

'I . . .' Taylor said.

I waited politely.

'Goodbye,' he finished, and strode out.

115

* * *

We kept the train song going for fifteen more minutes. During that time we had a couple of verses sung just by the girls, a couple just by the boys, a 'drum' solo from the whiteboard marker players and another from the chairs. When we finished, everyone clapped and applauded our success, then slumped down into their seats, glowing with the fun of it all.

'Okay, you all just chill out there for a moment,' I said. 'I'll play you something of a relaxing nature.'

I picked up the autoharp – an American old-time instrument, sort of a cross between a harp and an accordion – and played the old Scottish ballad, 'Black is the Colour'. It is one of the first folk songs I ever learned, and remains one of my favourites.

Black is the colour of my true love's hair
Her lips are like some roses fair
She's got the sweetest eyes and the gentlest hands
And I love the ground whereon she stands.

I received a gentle clap when I finished, not out of lack of enthusiasm, just because everyone was so content and mellow.

'Before we pack up for the night, would anyone else like to sing something?' I asked. 'I'm not forcing ye at all, but now that your musical muscles are kind of warmed up . . .'

'I'd like to,' a voice said, and there was Gladys, with her hand up.

'Great,' I said. 'Would you like me to back you?'

'If you want to,' she said.

'Okay, well, you just start and I'll fall in.'

She settled in her seat, closed her eyes, and began to sing.

Oh the snow it melts the soonest when the winds begin
*   to sing*

116

And the corn it ripens fastest when the frosts are setting
* in*
And when a young man tells me that my face he'll soon
* forget*
Before we part, I'd better croon, he'd be fain to follow
* it yet.*

I found her key easily (she sang the song in B flat) and simply affected a strum on the autoharp, which suited the old English folk song perfectly. Gladys had a wonderful lilting voice with a natural tremolo that was not intrusive. The song is about (as so many are) lost love and the fleeting nature of happiness. It struck me profoundly, as I played along on my autoharp, itself an instrument invented in the Victorian era and a favourite of English players of that time, that the song Gladys was sharing with us could easily have been played on the ancient pianoforte I had come across in the Blaney house. Our vocalist paused for a moment, nodding for me to play a solo. I obliged, and she finished with a refrain of the first verse. This time, no one held back on the applause.

'You are very, very talented,' I told Gladys as we finished. 'Where in the name of God did you learn to sing like that?'

'My mam and dad are both singers. My dad plays the melodeon, as well. I always picked up songs since I was little. As me parents got older the sessions in the house stopped,' she laughed. 'I haven't had an evenin' like this in a long time!'

There was general agreement to that.

'Well I want to hear more of your voice,' I said. 'And I want to hear Biddy play that accordion. But for tonight, that's all we have time for.'

I watched Gladys leave that evening, and there seemed to be an added spring to her step and a glow about her. I hoped the experience, and the fact that she had taken a chance on singing and it had paid off, would bolster her self-esteem and pay dividends in the weeks and months to come.

I came out of the classroom laden down with instrument cases, and found Jessie waiting for me.

'You all right, Jess?' I asked.

'Would you like me to carry some of those for you?' she asked.

'That'd be nice. Grab the uke – yeah, the small one – and the bag with the percussion gear in it. That's great, thanks.'

We walked towards the car.

'Can I ask you something?' Jessie inquired.

'Of course.'

'If someone you know is carrying on in a way that isn't right, but that person is sorta extra vulnerable – should you turn a blind eye or should you do something about it?'

'Jess, you've lost me I'm afraid,' I said. 'You're going to have to be a little less cryptic.'

We'd reached my car now and I opened the boot quickly and started to put the instruments in.

'Maybe the best thing for you to do would be to look at this,' Jessie said, taking out her phone.

I paused, my guitar half in and half out of the car.

'Are you about to show me a rather racy text message?' I asked.

Jessie froze, clearly amazed.

'How did you know that?'

'Sometimes I amaze myself,' I said drolly. 'And do you either suspect or know that the sender of that message is a person most often seen on a set of wheels.'

'I do,' Jessie said.

'Let's just say that this isn't the first time our friend's phone antics have been brought to my attention,' I said.

'You're not serious!' Jessie said, getting annoyed. 'He seems so harmless. I felt sorry for him.'

'Did you give him your number?'

'I did – he came up to me in the library, wanted to know how to use their online system to put aside a book. He's always on his own, y'know.'

I suddenly realized we were being watched. It was just a sensation at first, but then I caught a flash of movement and, peering into the shadows, I spotted Jeff McKinney trying to shrink back farther into the dark.

'I can see you, Jeff,' I shouted over at him. 'Either come out and face us or kindly fuck off.'

I waited, and it seemed he had gone, skulking away around the back of the school building.

'He is one weird puppy,' Jessie said, shuddering.

'I think it's time I had a word with Mr Taylor,' I said. 'Our Jeffie is starting to make quite the nuisance of himself.'

'I'd prefer it if you didn't mention my name,' Jessie said.

'Oh,' I said. 'Do you mind my asking why?'

'He's in a wheelchair . . .' Jessie said. 'It seems a bit wrong to complain about him.'

'Would you prefer he continue sending you obscene texts?' I said.

'No,' she said firmly.

'I'll see what I can do,' I said. 'But unless you're willing to come forward, I'm not sure what can really be done.'

I had a definite feeling I was being watched when I got home, but if Jeff was there, he was well hidden.

17

Despite everything, I slept like a log that night. Or at least, I slept like a log until about three, when I was awakened by someone kicking me – and not gently.

I had that moment of disorientation – how could I be so roughly awakened when I live alone – and reached over to switch on my bedside lamp. When the gloom was illuminated I was greeted by the sight of Lonnie Whitmore, dressed in his usual mismatched assortment of children's clothes and ill-fitting small adult wear, standing on my bed right beside me.

'Lonnie,' I said, my voice still thick with sleep, 'what the fuck, man? It's the middle of the night!'

My friend's response was to draw his leg back once again and deliver a crushing blow to my guts.

'Jesus Christ,' I gasped. 'What the hell is wrong with you?'

'You are a goddam asshole,' Lonnie said, leaning down so he was nose to nose with me. 'A useless' (kick), 'good for nothing' (kick), 'stupid hippy asshole!' Kick.

Completely winded, I rolled off the bed and onto the floor. It took me a couple of seconds to get air back into my lungs, but that was long enough for me to get the ends of the quilt wrapped about both hands. When I came up again I rapidly flung the duvet over my angry friend and bundled him up in it.

'You lousy shit,' he screamed, fighting like a miniature tiger. 'I'll fucking kill you.'

'You had your chance, Chucky,' I said, and hefting the weight of the bundle, I swung it into the wall with a pleasing thud. That shut him up.

'Okay,' I said, 'Are you finished being difficult, or do we go a couple of rounds more?'

'Fuck you,' came the meek response.

'Your choice, Mini Me,' I said, picking up the duvet for another swing, this time at the door, perhaps.

'Okay! Okay, I'll come nicely,' Lonnie bawled.

'You disappoint me,' I said, undoing the knot I had tied and releasing my visitor.

'You don't fight fair,' he said.

'Look, you caught me while I was asleep,' I reminded him. 'That is surely the very definition of fighting dirty.'

Lonnie accepted that truth begrudgingly.

'Fix me a drink,' he said. 'We need to talk.'

I poured him a dram of whiskey, and one for myself, and we sat in the living room in the semi-darkness.

'So to what do I owe this unexpected pleasure?' I asked. 'I mean, don't think that I don't enjoy you coming into my room in the middle of the night to try and beat me to death, but, y'know, sometimes it's nice to get a phone call first.'

'You really don't know why I'm mad?'

'No. I don't.'

'Do you remember the last time we spoke I suggested you keep a weather eye on the Blaney family?'

'Yeah. I have been.'

'You have been?'

'Yes. I have.'

'In what way, exactly?'

'I have been looking into things.'

'And what have you learned?'

'It looks very much like one or both parents are beating the kids.'

Lonnie made a 'get on with it' motion with one of his hands. 'And?'

'And the kids are dirty.'

'And?'

'And hungry.'

'And are they attending school?'

'They're getting home schooled.'

'Right. And would you say that you have been out at the house at all hours of the day – early morning, lunchtime, mid afternoon, evening . . .'

'Yeah. I suppose.'

'And during that time, have you ever seen any lessons going on?'

'C'mon, Lonnie. You know as well as I do that home schooling doesn't work that way.'

'It's indicative though, isn't it?'

'Indicative of what?'

'That those children are being left to stew in their own juices!'

'No, it does not mean that!'

'Come on, Shane! You know that what I'm saying is true. Twelve months ago, you'd have been out there with a team of social workers and whipped those children into care without thinking twice about it.'

'Maybe I would.'

'So what's holding you back now?'

'All those times I did that – every time I sailed in and did my knight on a white charger thing – did it ever really do any good?'

'Of course it did!'

'See, that's where we differ. I think I got way ahead of myself, and started developing notions of grandeur, a sense of self-importance I really did not warrant. I'm not making that mistake again.'

'Yet you go out there with food, you play games with the kids, you go and talk to the school.'

'How do you know about that?'

'Shane, I'm dead! I know everything.'

'You do?'

'It goes with the territory.'

'You don't look any smarter.'

'Believe me, I am.'

'Prove it.'

'The Blaney children are in trouble, and they need some-body to help them. And I don't mean a moderate, not too serious kind of trouble. I mean that, if something isn't done fast, one of those children will die.'

'Now you're being overdramatic.'

'I am not.'

'You are, too.'

'No I'm not.'

'Are.'

I drained my glass and stood up.

'I'm going back to bed. Thanks for stopping by, but could you maybe send me a text or something – a white dove or whatever is appropriate in your circumstances – before your next manifestation. Some of us have to work, you know.'

'What are you going to do about the Blaneys?'

'I am going to go back to sleep and think about it in the morning. It's not as if I *haven't* been thinking about it.'

'I want a more definitive answer than that,' Lonnie said.

'Well you are not getting one. And stay the fuck out of my room, will you? It's fucking creepy you keeping on showing up the way you have been.'

'I can make my presence felt from out here too, you know,' Lonnie shouted as I closed the door and went back to bed.

I assumed he meant he could get furniture to move on its own, but he didn't. He regaled me with his own utterly tuneless rendition of the entire album *Never Mind the Bollox* by The Sex Pistols. Somehow I got to sleep about five. As usual, the all-singing, all-dancing Lonnie was gone when I awoke.

18

I had arranged to go out to the Blaney house the following morning. Despite my restless night, I was up just after seven and set about making a picnic, trying to include as many different items as I could. I had bought a proper picnic basket (a good-sized one) after my last visit with the kids, and I filled it with a variety of sandwiches: I remembered from my time in residential care that egg mayonnaise was always a popular option, so I made some of those as well as ham and some cheese and tomato. I made lemonade which I put in large plastic bottles and packed into a cooler. I had baked an apple pie and made some cupcakes with butter icing, and this time I brought some grapes, plums and pears for the fruit course. Congratulating myself on the preparation of such a fine feast, I carried it out to the car.

At nine I strolled to the newsagents around the corner from my house. Garshaigh did not have a real arts supply shop, but the little shop at which everyone bought their newspapers sold various types of paper, paints, colouring books and drawing pads of all kinds. I bought a large blank art pad, some crayons, markers and chalks. Now I was ready for my visit.

Dora met me at the door.

'We're seein' a lot of you lately,' she said.

'Just trying to get to know you,' I said. 'I don't feel I can really write about someone until I have some sense of who they are.'

'Fair enough,' she said, standing back to let me in. 'Tom is away on business.'

'That's okay,' I said. 'The story isn't just about him, is it? It's about all of you.'

She thought about that.

'I promised him I'd clear one of the back rooms – he wants to use it as an office to deal with this whole bloody court case.'

'How's that proceeding?'

'I thought you'd have a better handle on that than me. Your boss seems pretty obsessed with it.'

'Oh, he's fascinated, all right,' I said. 'But he only tells me what he thinks I need to know.'

'Well, maybe I should take a leaf out of his book.'

'I won't tell,' I said, winking – Shane the charmer.

'I suppose it can't hurt. According to Tom his brother has produced a document – and Tom has seen a copy of it – written by a psychiatrist from the local sanatorium, swearing that his father was in mental distress when he made his final will. And apparently the psychiatrist is prepared to stand up in court and back this all up.'

'And is he reliable?' I asked. 'Some of those shrinks are as crazy as their patients.'

'From what I gather, this guy is not a nut job. Tom is up in a heap. *Saying* you have something is one thing, but *producing* it is a whole other thing. And then having the psychiatrist be happy to stand up and state his case – according to our guy, it gives Gerry a very strong case.'

'What will you do if you have to sell up?'

'Tom will never sell up,' Dora said dolefully. 'He'll barricade himself in here with his gun and that will be that. It'll be a fucking siege.'

'Let's hope it doesn't come to that,' I said.

'Maybe it's what we all need – a bit of a shake-up,' she said, but then seemed to catch herself and paused. 'I really have to sort out that room. Do you want to see the kids? The three youngest are about.'

'That'd be nice,' I said.

Winnie, Dom and Emma said they knew a great spot for a picnic and they led me across the fields for a couple of hundred yards until we came to a thicket of ash trees. What looked like a rabbit path had been beaten through these and Emma tripped down it, followed by the other two. All three children were barefoot, both girls wearing their grey/white shift dresses, Dom in the same clothes he had worn the last time I'd seen him. Emma led the way, weaving a path through the tall trees and leading us out into a hollow grove of bracken and gorse. A sheer wall of rock rose up behind, making the place sheltered and quiet, the sound of the trees rustling in the gentle breeze a pleasing ambient white noise.

I had brought a proper picnic blanket and laid it out on the soft grass, and Winnie insisted on helping me set the food and drink out.

'Who maked all this food?' Dom asked as we ate – it was only about 10.30 in the morning, but I hadn't had breakfast, and I assumed (correctly) that the children hadn't either, so everyone was quite happy to get stuck in.

'I did,' I said.

'You don't gots a wife?'

I shook my head.

'She dead?' Winnie asked.

'No,' I said. 'I just haven't got married yet, that's all.'

'You should get a wife for yourself,' Dom said, as if this was the most sensible thing in the world.

'Maybe I like being on my own,' I said.

'But if you had a wife, she could make your food,' Emma said, placing a hand on my arm as if to say: *this is very simple stuff you know – try and keep up!*

'You're all *eating* my food,' I said. 'Is it so bad that I need someone else to make it for me?'

There was much shaking of heads and noing to this question.

'Well, if I can make food that tastes good, and if I don't mind doing it – where's the problem?'

Winnie cut herself a huge slice of apple pie.

'What 'bout cleanin' up?' she asked. 'You surely to goodness can't like cleanin' up?'

'No,' I admitted. 'I don't really like cleaning. But when it's only me and Millie . . .'

'Who's Millie then?' Dom cut in.

'Millie is my dog.'

'What kind of a dog?'

'A greyhound,' I said.

'Do you race her?' Dom asked, his eyes lighting up.

'No.'

'Do you take her lamping?'

'No.'

'Do she go hare coursing?'

'No.'

The three children looked at me as if I were clearly intellectually disabled.

'Why do you have her then?' Dom asked, his voice dripping with disdain.

'She's my friend. I like the company.'

'D'you have any other friends?' Winnie wanted to know.

'I have you guys.'

'We don't count,' Dom said. 'We're just kids.'

'Yeah, I've got lots of friends,' I said, dodging the topic. A debate on Lonnie and my running away didn't seem useful. 'What about you? Do *you* have lots of friends?'

'Nah,' Emma said, shoving half a cupcake into her mouth. 'We ain't allowed to play with other kids, in case they teaches us bad stuff.'

'There must be other kids who don't watch TV and live like you do,' I said. 'Maybe you could play with them?'

'Jimmy used to go t' school,' Winnie said. 'I hoped they'd let me go, but they di'n't. Dad said Jim had been ruint by goin'.'

'I bet your mum teaches you loads though,' I said. 'I'm sure she makes your lessons really fun.'

'She never teaches us nothin',' Emma said. ' "You go on out an' play, children, while I clean up in here." That's what she says.'

'She must teach you *sometimes*,' I said.

'I don't remember the last time,' Dom said. 'Winnie can barely read, and I can just about write my name. Emma there can't read at all!'

'Is that true, Emma?' I asked.

'I can sing you the alphabet,' Emma offered, not one bit embarrassed at these revelations. 'Jim teached me.'

She stood up and began to sing the Alphabet song most children learn at school. I could tell that she had learned it phonetically – the letters themselves meant nothing to her. 'L, M, N, O, P' became 'ellemellohpee' and 'Q, R, S' was sung as 'queues are best'. But I applauded loudly when she finished.

'So I can *kind* of read,' Emma said, getting some more lemonade.

When we had cleared away the food I took the paper and colouring materials from another bag.

'Here's something for you all,' I said. 'Let's draw some pictures.'

The kids pounced on the colours delightedly.

'What of?' Dom asked.

'Anything you like,' I said.

The next hour was spent with me idly sketching the ash grove, while the three children filled page after page with images. I paid no attention, not wanting to staunch their creativity in any way. I hate seeing children being given a page with a picture already on it – that has its place, but true creativity begins with an empty page and no limits placed on what can go on it. The kids, who usually chatted away nineteen to the dozen, fell silent and all I could hear was the scratching of pens on paper, bird song from above and the trees whispering to us all.

As the time on my watch approached midday, I called a halt.

'All right you lot,' I said. 'I have to get back to work, and your mother will think that I have abducted you all. Let's have a look at what you drew.'

'I drawed our house,' Emma said, showing me a very colourful rendition of the homestead, with a smiling sun in the sky above it. 'That's me in the window, waving.'

There was a little stick figure in the top right window, waving out.

'And who's this?' I asked, pointing to another window, in which was a rather frightening-looking face.

'That's Bad Daddy,' Emma said.

'Bad Daddy?'

'Yeah. We have a Good Daddy and a Bad Daddy.'

This was new.

'Like, two different people?'

'No!' Winnie said. 'The same. But different too. Look.'

She produced a page which had been divided into two equal parts by a line down the middle. On one side was a figure that was certainly Tom. It was big, lumpy, dressed in a blue shirt and jeans, with a mess of black hair and a smiling face. Behind him was the house, again with a sunny sky, clouds and birds. On the other was the same blue-clad figure, but this time with a fiercely angry face. The background showed black clouds and lightning, and in Bad Daddy's hand was a stick or cudgel.

'I see,' I said. 'I take it you don't like Bad Daddy much.'

'He'll whip you,' Dom said.

He showed me a picture he had drawn of a large figure, hand raised above his head, while a smaller one cowered.

'An' he'll do worse stuff,' Winnie said gravely.

She held up a picture of a room where a black figure stood at the door. In the room was a bed, with the blankets clumped up. The occupant was not on the mattress, but hiding underneath, a common defensive tactic for children whose nights are disturbed by abusers.

'Yeah, we got a Bad Daddy an' a Good Daddy,' Emma said, laughing. 'Course, Mammy is just Mammy. Not good, not bad, jus' Mammy.'

I doubted if that was much of a comfort.

19

I asked the kids if I could bring the pictures with me. They agreed so long as I let them hold on to the paper and pens. I said I thought it a perfect swap.

That afternoon I had to attend a trade union gathering, but I found it very difficult to focus. The pictures the children had drawn kept swimming round in my head. To my huge relief the meeting ended just after five and I went home to find Millie asleep in the kennel I had got for her. I put her in the back of the car and we went out to the beach where I jogged for a couple of miles, an activity that made me want to throw up, but at least drove thoughts of dual personality daddies out of my head for half an hour.

I cooked some steak for dinner, then sat down in front of *Starsky and Hutch* (the original series, of course) on the crime network. A kid with special needs was witness to a robbery and was being bullied not to testify. The two detectives were getting rather emotional about protecting him. I knew how they felt.

I don't remember going to get the whiskey, but by the time Lonnie showed up I was roaring drunk.

'So what's your excuse this time?' he asked.

' 'Scuse?'

'What's your excuse for not going to the police or social services or whatever the fuck?'

' 'Bout what?'

'The Blaney children! You now have solid evidence that they are being abused.'

'Don't.'

'You fucking do!'

'The pictures do not show anyone being 'bused. They could just show the kids are scared of their Dad. It isn' enough.'

'You asshole!' Lonnie screamed and punched me full force in the face. I was too stunned to speak for a moment, then gathered myself and lunged at him, but he was right across the other side of the room by the time I was able to move.

'You fucking shithead!' I roared. 'You call me a chicken? You say I'm not fulfilling my respons'bilities? You went and fucking died on me! You ran out on me, and then you turn up as some crazy brain episode I'm having, and you have the balls to call me a coward? *You* left *me*! So don't come the high 'n' mighty, Lonnie Whitmore. It doesn't wash.'

'Those kids have no one.'

'Oh my God, Lonnie – every case I get involved in, they *always* have no one. I'm listening to that all my life – *you're the only one that can help* – well guess what? I'm not! There are plenty of other people out there. I'm a journalist now, and a teacher. I don't need this shit in my head anymore.'

'Christ on a bike, this is rich coming from you. Mister high and mighty! I actually thought you were worth something. I thought you were the man! But you are just a long-haired bleeding-heart wimp. That is all you are.'

'Fuck off Lonnie. Go back to wherever you go when you're not pissing me off.'

'You don't get off that lightly. This is not about some

abstract moral dilemma. Those children are real, real kids who are probably hurting right this minute.'

'*Do you think I don't know that?*' I screamed at him.

Millie whined and ran under the couch.

'*Do you think I don't see those pictures in my head even as I am talking to you? After all that we've been through together, do you believe that I can just pass that off as meaningless?*'

'So do something about it!' Lonnie bellowed back, standing up on the arm of the chair. 'Make a difference in those kids' lives.'

'*I can't!*'

'Why not?'

'Because I'm afraid!'

'What of?'

'Of getting dragged back into all that shit again. The emotions and the pain and the constant possibility that you are *fucking up* someone's life for good. I am *tired* of all that, Lonnie. Why do you think I came here in the first place?'

'I don't know about all that shit,' Lonnie said, levelling his finger at me. 'But I do know this: *you cannot pussy out on those kids*. They need you, and *you* owe *me*. If our friendship ever meant anything to you, prove it. Show me what kind of a man you really are.'

I gazed at him, stunned at what we had both just said, but particularly sickened that he would play that card.

'I cannot believe you just said that,' I murmured, my words barely audible.

'Believe it. You know what you have to do,' Lonnie Whitmore said, and then he wasn't there anymore. I sat on the couch, my dog quivering with fear beneath me, and cried.

The girl was quiet. It was as if something had extinguished a light in her.

'What's wrong?' I asked. She was kneeling on the ground, plucking the petals from a daisy one at a time.

'Nothin'.'

'You seem unhappy.'

'I'm a'right, Ya can' be happy all de time, can ye?'

'Well, that's true,' I said. 'But usually you want to play and you like to have a chat and to show me interesting places in the fields and in the woods. Today you just seem to not want to do anything. And that's not like the person you usually are.'

'Maybe I'm tired today. Or maybe I has a pain in my tummy.'

'Do you?'

'Not in my tummy.'

'But you do have a pain?'

Without looking back at me, she held out her wrist, which was bruised almost black.

'How'd you do that, sweetie?'

'It just happened.'

'I bet it hurts, right?'

She nodded.

'I have some painkillers in my car. I can get them.'

'What they?'

'Um – tablets? Medicine?'

'Make de pain go 'way?'

'Hopefully, yes.'

'Daddy won't mind, will he?'

'I'll talk to him, or your mum,' I said. 'Do they know about your wrist?'

'Daddy does, anyway.'

'Does he?'

She turned and rested her head on my shoulder.

'Maybe if my arm gets better from your medicine, maybe then we could play some games or go fer a walk.'

'If you like,' I said. 'But you know, sometimes it's fun to just be still and watch the clouds. Did you ever play Cloud Shapes?'

'No. What's that?'

I picked her up and put her sitting on my shoulders.

'Let's get those painkillers, and then I'll show you how to play.'

She proved to be very good at it.

20

Robert Chaplin held his head in his hands and said nothing for a long time. I wondered if he might have gone to sleep. But after what seemed like an age he said:

'This is going to fuck everything up.'

'I don't follow.'

'You go to social services with your evidence and they take the kids into care. Of course, Tom Blaney will know it was you, and the entire bunch of them will refuse to deal with the *Western News*, and who could blame them. This – the biggest story of my career – falls asunder. Brilliant.'

'It doesn't have to work that way,' I said.

'Paint me a different picture then,' Chaplin said.

'There is no guarantee the kids will be taken into care. The evidence is kind of vague. I still believe that we are dealing with neglect and physical abuse, but the sexual stuff is by no means definitive. I think it far more likely that a Family Support Worker will be asked to visit a few hours a week. That's a person whose job it is to teach about nutrition, hygiene, behaviour management – that kind of thing. I also think the family will be asked to connect the electricity and the mains water, and to send the kids to school. From what I can gather the children are barely literate.'

'What you are describing is as much the death of my story as the other way. What you are suggesting could happen will be the end of the Blaneys' distinct character. If they stop living that strange life of theirs, half their mystique vanishes.'

'You understand that I cannot leave the children in danger.'

'Of course I do! It was always going to be a risk when I hired you – god-awful bloody do-gooders! Can't keep your nose out of anyone's business!'

'I can also make the referral anonymously.'

Chaplin perked up a bit.

'You can?'

'I can explain my circumstances and ask that my name be kept out of things. That way, the Blaneys need never know it was me who called it in.'

Chaplin rubbed his eyes.

'Well do it that way then, please. It'll still be touch and go, though – remember, the Blaneys fucking own this town. They'll more than likely find out.'

Part of me – a big part – thought Chaplin was probably right.

But I left the office and made the referral anyway.

21

Child services were based in an old hospital a mile out of town on the Galway side. I told the girl at the counter why I was there and waited as she talked quietly into a phone.

'Someone will be with you shortly,' she said.

They weren't. I had my Lee Child book with me and had three chapters half read – I was too antsy to concentrate on it properly – before I heard my name being called. Standing at the counter was a broad man of about my own age with a shaved head and a thick reddish-brown moustache. He was dressed in a grey sports coat over a T-shirt with the Batman logo on it and blue jeans.

'I'm Sid Doran, the duty social worker,' he said, taking my hand and shaking it, but not really making eye contact. The duty social worker is the person who sits at the end of the phone, answering and recording all calls that come into the child protection offices. He organizes the initial investigations and decides if a case requires further intervention.

'Thanks for seeing me,' I said.

He brought me to a small office and we sat.

'How can I help you today?' Sid asked, opening a yellow legal pad and taking an expensive-looking pen from his breast pocket.

'I am sure you are aware of the Blaney family,' I began, and told him about my concerns, about how the children had indicated that they were not getting fed regularly, about Dom's bruises, about what the principal of the primary school had said, and then I took out the pictures and gave him a commentary on Good Daddy/Bad Daddy.

Sid listened and took copious notes, pausing occasionally to ask questions or to get me to go back over something he had not understood fully. Because I had kept track of all visits for the newspaper, I had dates and times on everything.

'That is incredibly thorough,' the social worker said when I was finished.

'I worked as a child protection worker in one form or another for most of my life,' I told him.

'Why the change of career?'

'I'm going to be honest and say burnout,' I forced a smile.

Sid sat back and looked over the pages he had written.

'Pretend you had just caught this case,' he said. 'I mean, you've been around this family quite a bit by the sound of it. What's your gut instinct about what's going on?'

'Well, my gut tells me there is most definitely *something* going on,' I said. 'I wouldn't be here if I didn't think that.'

'Yeah, but go beyond that. Get specific for me. Take this Good Daddy/Bad Daddy thing. Looking back on the time you've been out at the house, would you say the children are afraid of their father?'

'I would say that the only child who has any real relationship with him is the eldest boy, Jim. The others are pretty indifferent to him. But you see, isn't it possible they have created a situation where they can separate the man from the actions? When he's nice, he's Good Daddy, and therefore kind of harmless. When he's bad, he's Bad Daddy and he does awful things – but Bad Daddy is a different entity to Good

140

Daddy. If you're angry with him or afraid of him, you're *not* angry or afraid of Good Daddy. I think in their world, where they don't see anyone other than the immediate family, these children have created a way of coping with the fact that their dad has some serious issues.'

'But you never saw him do anything inappropriate?'

'I thought getting Jim to hit that guy who had come out to warn them off was sort of inappropriate.'

'But within certain cultural frameworks it was understandable.'

'You can explain almost anything away using that argument.'

'Perhaps.'

Sid continued to go over his notes.

'I'd like my name kept out of things for the time being,' I said. 'I am involved with the family in my capacity as a journalist, and I'd like to continue in that vein. I will, of course, continue to pass any relevant information on to yourselves.'

Sid seemed not to have heard me. His eyes were still on his pages of writing.

'Sid, did you get that?' I asked.

He looked up sharply.

'Yes, of course. I'm sure we can do that for the time being. Thanks so much for stopping in.'

I was a bit nonplussed.

'Is that it?'

'I may have to call you again, but for now, I think we're done.'

He stood. I did too, and shook his hand.

'We'll be in touch if we need anything else,' Sid said again as he waved me out the door.

I drove off feeling like I had made a serious mistake. Chaplin's dagger-like gaze, which was waiting when I got back to the office, didn't make me feel any better.

22

I had bitten the bullet, and figured that my best course of action was now to focus on the things I was supposed to be doing, like working for the newspaper, teaching my classes and perhaps putting some effort into making the house I had moved into a home: it had remained little more than a shell in the months since I had arrived.

Chaplin's jealously took the Blaney story as even more of a personal quest. Books on local history and even an ancient tome on the Ponse de Blaney clan formed a solid wall about his desk. He barely spoke to me, simply barking instructions as to where he wanted me to go and what he wanted me to write. One day it was an obituary for a local sporting hero, the next a double-page spread on a shoplifting epidemic in the town centre. I took it all in good spirits and tried to invest every item with some enthusiasm and a sense of the dramatic. I developed a style not unlike that which Stan Lee had used in the Marvel comics of the sixties and seventies, all heavy alliteration and pregnant pauses. I received no complaints from Chaplin, so assumed it was going down reasonably well with the readers.

In the evenings Millie and I explored the highways and

byways around Garshaigh. We would get into the car and drive until we were lost, then get out and walk for an hour in as straight a line as we could manage. I found the countryside rich with wildlife, alive with history. My greyhound and I found old round towers, badger setts that stretched for a quarter of a mile, and a colony of roe deer living in an old apple grove near the ruins of a Georgian manor.

As I took the paper more seriously, I began to see why the local people might protest at an attempt to turn this landscape into an urban sprawl. Gerry Blaney, it appeared, might truly be the Machiavelli Chaplin painted him as.

One day in early December I was having lunch in the café when Carla, who had come to refill my coffee mug, nodded at the window.

'I think someone wants to see you,' she said.

Looking up, I realized that Gladys Pointer was standing by the door outside, gazing in but looking uncomfortable.

'She there long?' I asked.

'Maybe ten minutes. Want me to run her?'

'No. I'll ask her in. She obviously has something on her mind.'

Gladys didn't even pretend she wasn't looking for me.

'Thought you'd never ask!' she said when I stuck my head out the door.

We sat down and my companion ordered a hot chocolate with marshmallows.

'So what has you hanging about out in the cold trying to catch my attention?' I asked. 'We've class in two days' time – what can't wait until then?'

'I wanted to get you on your own,' Gladys said. 'I wish *she* wasn't here,' this directed at Carla, 'but I suppose I'll have to make do.'

'Carla is busy,' I said, patting her on the hand. 'She won't be listening to anything we say. So, come on then – what's the story?'

'Okay. You gave me a lot of praise the other night when I sang.'

'It wasn't empty praise, either,' I said. 'I wasn't trying to butter you up or anything of that nature. You were amazing.'

She grinned and flushed a bit.

'You're a good teacher,' she said.

'Now who's buttering who up?' I said, laughing.

'No. You are. You're the best teacher I ever had.'

'I don't think you had a very good time at school, Gladys, did you?'

'I fuckin' hated it,' she said.

'That was probably partly because of your own unwillingness to be there, and maybe you had one or two unsympathetic teachers along the way,' I said. 'But look, you're back now and you're liking it. That's good, right?'

She took a spoonful of mushy marshmallows. I knew she had something important to say. She would get to it in her own time.

'I told you how in school they said I was dumb.'

'You did.'

'Well, you never treat me like that. You talk to me just like everyone else, you make me think I can do anything I want.'

'That's because you can. You are a smart young woman.'

'See, there you're wrong. I'm not.'

'Of course you are! Why would you say you're not?'

'I'm not like the rest of them girls, Shane. I *am* thick. Really, really stupid.'

'Stop, Gladys, for God's sake,' I said, getting annoyed. 'Has someone been giving you a hard time?'

She shook her head and continued to consume her frothy,

gloopy drink. I was always amazed at her capacity to have conversations like this while continuing with whatever else was going on. It was always like such momentous things were secondary concerns.

'I can't read, Shane,' she said, looking me dead in the eye for the first time. 'I have never gotten the hang of it, and now I'm doing this course and we have project work due and I can't do none of it.'

I sat back and considered what she'd said.

'You can't read at all?'

'Oh, a little bit,' she said, clearly vexed by the question. 'I can write my name and I can manage road signs and I can just about work my way about a menu in a chip shop.'

'So you know your letters and you can recognize words and syntax – the order words need to go in a sentence.'

'Yeah,' she stopped scooping out her unctuous beverage. 'What are you getting at?'

'You *can* read, then,' I said. 'You've just never tried to tackle something like a book, and I doubt you've ever read a magazine or a newspaper.'

'I can look up what's on TV in the little insert that comes around with the *News*,' she said. 'But that's as far as it goes.'

'Look, I'm not a literacy teacher,' I said. 'There are people specially trained to work with people with those kinds of difficulties. But I'll tell you what – you come around to the class an hour before kick-off this week, and we'll take a look at your reading ability and see if we can't help you a little bit.'

'D'you think you can?'

'I have no idea,' I said. 'What I do know is that it's probably nowhere near as bad as you think it is, and that school can sometimes be a really scary experience for kids – it can put them off things for the rest of their lives. Look at me: I can barely do simple maths because of something a teacher put in my school report once – put me off numbers for ever. So I do know where you're coming from.'

Gladys sniffed, and I saw that, despite her attempts to be dispassionate, she was actually crying quietly.

'So maybe I'm not dumb after all?'

I took her hand and squeezed it.

'One thing I am absolutely, categorically certain of miss, is that you are in no way, shape or form dumb. And I want you to stop saying it. You have to start believing in yourself.'

'I'll try.'

'You're going to have to do better than that,' I said.

'Little baby steps,' Gladys said, but she smiled and wiped her eyes.

It was a start.

23

A week passed since I had gone to social services, then two. I waited for Chaplin to storm into the offices of the *Western News*, informing me that it was all over, that social workers had stormed the house like a battalion of the SAS, and the entire family had been whisked off to various care institutions. But nothing of the sort happened, and my boss remained implacable.

I knew from experience that things can move painstakingly slowly in the field of child protection. Cases can take years to come to a climax; however, I also knew that there would have been a visit to the house within, at the most, forty-eight hours of my visiting Sid Doran. Taking that into consideration, Chaplin should have seen some changes, even if only in the moods of the parents.

Finally, I could stand the suspense no longer.

'Rob, can I ask you something?'

'No.'

'You've been out to the Blaney house within the last few days, yeah?'

'I refuse to tell you anything about the Blaney family on grounds that you are likely to stick your busy-bodying, bleeding-heart do-gooder nose into things and make a complete fuck-up of my life.'

'Yeah, I know all that, but you have, haven't you?'

Chaplin sighed a deep 'will he never relent' sort of sigh.

'I was out there yesterday. A date has been set for the hearing. Tom is like a bear with a sore head over it all.'

'But other than that, you didn't notice any difference? Dora made no reference to social services being out . . . the kids didn't look cleaner or better fed?'

'They all looked exactly the same to me, which is how I like it, thank you very fucking much.'

'They shouldn't, though,' I said.

'Look, as much as it has pissed me off, you did the right thing. Obviously the other do-gooders down the social decided that you didn't have enough to bring them out there. Boo hoo. Very sad. Think of it this way: there must be other, needier children that require attention.'

I said nothing, turning back to my keyboard and finishing a piece I was writing. Chaplin was probably right. Probably.

Half an hour later I made an excuse ('I need to pick up an ink cartridge, Rob,') and made for my car.

At child services, the same girl was behind the counter, looking as if she had never left. I wondered if she slept in the cupboard behind her.

'Could I see Sid Doran please?'

'And do you have an appointment sir?'

'No. I came here two weeks ago to make a referral, and I just wanted to follow up on that.'

'Very well, just take a seat and I'll see what I can do.'

I sat in the same chair I had occupied during my last visit. I again tried to read (this time Garth Ennis's *Preacher*) but made comparable headway.

After fifteen minutes a tall, thin woman in black skinny

jeans and a grey woollen top arrived at the counter, whispered something to the blonde girl and approached me.

'Mr Dunphy, I'm Josephine Welch, senior social worker. Thank you for taking the time to call out. I assure you that the matter is fully in hand.'

'The family have been visited?'

'Your concerns have been addressed. Thank you for your time.'

I realized she was more or less telling me to leave. I wasn't going to go so easily.

'I used to be a social care worker. I know that, as the person who made the complaint, I am entitled to an update on what you've done.'

'As I said, we are dealing with your issues. That really is as much as I can divulge just now.'

'Have you called out to the house or not?'

'Goodbye, Mr Dunphy.'

Josephine Welch turned on her heel and walked back the way she had come. I sat there for another five minutes, but no more information was forthcoming. I considered chaining myself to the chair, but it wasn't bolted to the floor and was made of fairly flimsy plastic.

And I didn't have any chains. The world just kept on throwing obstacles in my way.

'You got a mammy and daddy?'

'My mammy is dead,' I said.

'Oh!' she was genuinely shocked by this news. It was as if the mortality of her parents had never occurred to her.

'You sad 'bout dat?'

'I was. I still miss her, but I'm not as sad as I used to be.'

'Your daddy alive still?'

'Yes.'

'Him sad?'

'He was, too, but he got married again to a very nice woman.'

'So . . . you gots a new mammy . . .'

'I suppose I do. But I was a grown-up when my dad married her, so as much as I am fond of her she's not really like a mam to me – I don't need minding.'

'But she nice to you.'

'She is. Very much.'

The girl was picking up pebbles and putting them into groups based on their colour.

'Your daddy whack you?'

I thought about the question – it was a miracle I had never been asked it before during all my time working with children, but I hadn't. I was tempted to dodge it, but then decided on the truth.

'Well, when I was little it was very normal for parents to smack their children. My dad slapped me from time to time – never really very hard – and so did my mum.'

'They ever make you cry with them whacks?'

'I don't really remember,' I said. 'I reckon they must have done, but it didn't happen very often.'

'You mad at them for whackin' you?'

'No,' I said. 'They weren't being mean. I was usually being a bit of a brat. My brother was even worse, though. He used to be very badly behaved sometimes, and he'd get whacked a lot more than me.'

'What he do?' she asked, her voice hushed in fascination.

'Well, once, he told my mother to shut up!'

I realized as I said it that any other child would laugh in my face – dialogue between children and parents now regularly contained worse insults than that. But the girl gasped in horror.

'He tole her to shuddup! He must've been whacked somethin' dreadful!'

I laughed.

'I remember seeing him coming running out of our garden as fast as his little legs could carry him, and then I realized that my dad was running after him.'

'Oh no,' she said, her hands to her mouth, barely breathing.

'Well, it didn't take my dad long to catch him, and he got a wallop then. But, see, my parents didn't hit us and keep hitting us. We'd get a slap, usually on the bum, and that would be that. I think my brother got sent to bed really early that evening, but that was as far as it went.'

The girl's eyes were wide, her face pale.

'If I said that to my mammy or daddy, I'd be whacked so bad I couldn' walk fer a week,' she said.

'They wouldn't hit you that hard, would they?' I asked.

'Well, not my mam, but my dad? You can be sure he would

whack you and whack you. He uses him fists like dis—'

She bunched up her fists and snarled at me, punching the air like a boxer in training.

'And what about other punishments,' I asked. 'Do you ever get sent to bed early or grounded?'

'We gets sent to bed alrigh',' she said.

'I used to hate that,' I said. 'I'd look out the window at all my friends playing on the street outside, and I'd feel terribly lonely.'

'Oh,' the girl said, 'we don't be lonely. When we gets sent to bed, we isn't on our own for very long.'

She wouldn't be drawn on what she meant by that.

The conversation was closed.

24

I had never seen a child protection case from the outside before, and I was not enjoying the experience. I sat in the Austin, playing Tom Waits very loudly for five minutes so no one would hear me shouting and swearing. Then I drove far too fast back to the office. When Chaplin asked me if I had gotten the ink cartridge I simply glared at him, and we spent the rest of the afternoon staring at one another through lidded eyes. It was very silly and not very productive.

I was just about to tidy up before going home when my mobile phone rang.

'Sid Doran here,' came the voice. No beating about the bush with this guy.

'Thanks for getting back to me, Sid. I was just wondering if you made any progress on the Blaney situation?'

'Obviously I can't tell you too much – confidentiality and all that.'

'I just want to know if you checked out the issues I brought to your attention.'

'Yes. A home visit was made.'

'And?'

'All I am obligated to tell you is that we did make a follow-up visit.'

'Sid, I'm a journalist, and I have contacts within child services all over the country. I could make a few telephone calls, talk to a few administrators in your office – it would take me a bit longer, but I could certainly get the information. Wouldn't it be easier to just let me know what your plans are for the family?'

The line went quiet as Sid Doran thought about what I had said. I could almost hear the cogs grinding.

'I went out there with a colleague a week ago. We took all your worries on board and we spent quite some time with the children and interviewed both parents.'

'You didn't talk to the kids *in front* of the parents . . .'

'I am a fully trained professional, Shane, with quite a few years' experience.'

'Fair enough, I had to ask.'

'Granted. We did very definitely find some issue of concern. Many of them were points you had raised. But we did not consider some other factors to be of such a pressing nature. So we will be discussing those points we think need to be addressed with Tom and Dora, and I believe we can make some headway on those.'

'I see. So the kids won't be taken into care?'

'We did not see that as a necessity. In fact, I reckon it might actually have a negative effect. As you are aware, the likelihood of keeping the children together should they be placed in a residential setting would be very slim. These kids have a very powerful bond, Shane, which I would be loathe to break.'

'So will there be continued contact from your office?'

'We may appoint a worker. There are still some elements of our initial investigation outstanding. When it is complete we'll have a clearer picture.'

I wasn't sure how I felt about this news. On the face of it, I knew I should be pleased. But there was something niggling at me.

'Did you talk to the school?'

'I think I've said as much as I can,' Sid said in his deadpan way. 'Thanks for all your help on this, Shane. You did the right thing. The family definitely needs help. They'll all be better for it.'

'Thanks, Sid,' I said. 'We'll be in touch, yeah?'

'I'm sure we will,' he said, and hung up.

I had a feeling I had just been fobbed off, but knew that there wasn't a damn thing I could do about it. If Sid had been out a week ago, and Chaplin hadn't noticed any real difference, whatever social services had done had made little impression on them. That either meant that the Blaneys weren't taking the machinations of the child protection services seriously, or that they felt they could simply ignore them without any serious repercussions. Either way, it didn't look good.

Sid Doran struck me as a thorough, professional kind of guy. He did not look like someone who would allow Tom or any of his brother's thugs – or the family's not inconsiderable money and influence – frighten him. So what had happened?

I knew there was only one way to find out.

25

I got out to the Blaney house at eight thirty the next morning. A mist was coming in off the sea and I could hear herring gulls calling to one another as they rode thermals high above me. I had bought a cup of coffee in a foam cup at a service station on the way out and I sat where I was in the Austin, the window rolled down, sipping it, enjoying the early morning sights and sounds. I didn't know how well Tom would greet me – I was mindful of Chaplin's contention that he would find out that I had 'informed' on him – so was a little reluctant to get out and knock. The decision was taken out of my hands, however, when the large bulk of Tom Blaney hove into sight. He must have been walking the perimeter again.

'Can I help you with something?' he asked.

I searched for more hostility than usual in his voice, but could find none.

'Just making an early call,' I said. 'I've some stuff to do in Ennis later today, but I had it down in my notebook to drop out and see you, so I thought I'd fit you in before leaving. I always figured you for an early riser, what with the farm and all.'

That seemed to please him.

'Sure haven't I a day's work done already,' he said. 'You want to come in for a bit?'

I shrugged.

'I'll walk with you if that suits you better. I just want to run over what's happening with the case. I hear a date has been set. How's your side of things going?'

Something seemed to darken in him.

'Not so well. My legal team tell me we have little to go on. And that bastard Gerry is sinking lower and lower every day.'

'Yeah? What's he done now?'

Tom sighed and looked out towards the ocean.

'Come on in. I've somethin' I want to show you.'

He brought me into a room behind the living area, a dark, stuffy, windowless cell that was piled with papers and books, mostly of a legal or historical nature. He spent a minute or two lighting candles and oil lamps, then asked me to sit in an ornate-looking armchair.

'Would it not be better to use a room that has some natural light?' I asked, not unreasonably.

'I don't want to give anyone the option of looking in from the outside,' he said. 'This is my war room. I have to keep it as secret as I can. I'll spend money on a few candles if that's what it takes.'

'Fair enough,' I said.

Tom dug about in a drawer in a heavy wooden desk.

'This is my father,' he said, pushing a black-and-white photograph in a leather frame towards me. The image was of a square-jawed, determined-looking man with a shock of white hair and a quizzical eye.

'He looks like a smart man,' I said, not quite sure what the customary response was. 'He has real character in his face.'

'He was a great man,' Tom said. 'A really great man. I want you, a master of letters, to look over something and tell me

157

if it is the work of a person losing their wit. Gerry is alleging that my father was in the latter stages of dementia just before he died. Now, I can tell you that I spent almost every waking hour in his company, and I never had any sense of him not being in control or experiencing any kind of issues with memory or understanding. This is an addendum to his will – it was read out by the solicitor when the contents of the legal document were revealed to the family. It was penned two days before Da died.'

He held out a piece of heavy paper, folded many times.

'You're sure you want me to read it?' I asked. 'I mean, it's very personal.'

'Read it.' Tom said and, sitting down on the chair opposite me, folded his arms and closed his eyes as if going to sleep.

The letter carried the address of the Blaney home and was dated as Tom had indicated. It was handwritten in a deliberate, masculine script and looked as if it had been executed in fountain pen. I wondered if Chaplin had been shown this. I would have to ask him.

Dear Thomas,

The land is my greatest gift to you. It has sustained our family in this beautiful, mystical place for more than nine centuries, and I bequeath it to you now. Tend it. Till it. Feed it with your sweat and the sweat of your children. The land in the West is harsh and unforgiving. If you show weakness it will break you like a twig in the wind. I know I have sometimes been a cruel parent and an unloving father, but this has been because I need you to be strong and unyielding. My dearest wish is that, in another millennium, there will be the children of a Ponse de Blaney on these acres, living as we have lived, as our father lived and as his father lived. You hold the authority to achieve that now, Thomas. Do not let me down.

I am going to my grave in an era where the mind has no peace. I cast aside the trappings of modernity many years ago now, and it did my soul good to see you do likewise. Do not waver in your determination to continue in this fashion. The media peddles poison: sex, ignorance, crudity and disrespect for all things decent. My life has only been improved since I went back to traditional ways. I know you feel the same. Do not allow your children's minds and spirits to be warped by the smut and evil that abounds through television, radio and, worst of all, the internet. Teach them yourself, you and your wife, so you know precisely what they are learning.

I leave you my land, my house and the largest portion of my money. I have found that the best way to keep wealth is to be slow to spend it. On these acres, be they field, hill, beach or woodland, you will find everything you and your family need to live well. Make your way through what is free and to hand. Leave the money where it is, spend only what you need and you will find yourself never wanting.

Treat your brother well. He has chosen a different road to you – to us – but he is still your blood.

Make me proud, son. Make your forefathers proud,
Your loving father.

I couldn't read the signature, but then, I didn't need to. I looked over and saw that Tom was gazing at me.

'Well,' he said. 'Is he mad?'

'I would say that he comes across as a little eccentric,' I said delicately. 'But the letter is well structured, very articulate and follows a clearly laid-out theme. He knows exactly what he wants to say to you, and says it. There is no dementia evident, no.'

Tom leaped up as if I had just slapped him.

'I knew it! I knew it! Come on. Let's celebrate!'

He ran out of the room with a hop and skip, like a small boy. I followed, barely keeping up.

Tom went straight to one of the stairwells that plunged down under the earth into the basement tunnels.

'Come on,' he called back. 'You'll be glad you did.'

Using my phone as a torch, as I had done before, I went into the darkness. The corridors down here smelt of damp earth and must. I could just make out his dark shape ahead of me, but then it disappeared.

'Into your left,' he called, and then a blanket of light spilled out of a doorway, and I knew where I was going.

The room, when I got there, was full of barrels, all stacked up against the wall. He had a small table and two wooden chairs in the middle of the floor upon which were sat some pewter mugs.

'Sit, sit,' he said, picking up one of the mugs and opening a tap in one of the barrels that was sitting a little higher up the wall.

He placed the full mug in front of me. I picked it up and sniffed the contents. The aroma was malty, slightly sweet – altogether very pleasant.

'Drink,' he urged.

I took a sip. It was ale. And very good ale at that: it had a deep, hopsy flavour, lightly effervescent but not too gassy.

'Did you brew this yourself?'

'The barrels from here down are mine,' Tom said, indicating a spot on the wall. 'What you have was made by my father.'

'It is excellent,' I said. 'But look, I have to drive. How strong is it?'

'You have two mugs with me, and then I'll give you a bit of breakfast – you can go for a swim if you like too – and then you can be on your way.'

I reasoned that (seeing as my trip to Ennis was fictitious anyway) it couldn't do any real harm to have a few drinks with the man. So I raised my mug.

'To the Ponse de Blaneys,' Tom said solemnly.

'The Ponse de Blaneys,' I echoed and we drank.

'He set the fuckin' social workers on me you know,' Tom said after a few moments of contemplation.

'Who – your dad?' I asked, caught off guard.

'No. Fucking Gerry.'

'Tell me,' I said.

'They came out a week or so ago. A bald bloke and a skinny woman. Talked to the children, talked to Dora. Talked to *me*. Said that someone had voiced concerns. I mean, what does that even mean, eh?'

'Damned if I know,' I said, playing the innocent.

'I'll be the first to admit I slap the kids from time to time. It's how I was raised and it's the only way I know. I stand over my decision not to send them to school. You've spent time with my kids and you can testify that they are mannerly and well behaved.'

'Totally,' I said.

'There was some guff about them being too small – failure to thrive or some such shite. Of course they're small,' he laughed, the sound like a dog barking. 'They're kids! I mean to say, what do you expect?'

'So what's going to happen?' I asked, having another swallow of ale. I was already feeling a little light-headed – it was a very long time since I'd drunk before ten o'clock in the morning.

'I have to send them to school, the whole lot of them, even

Jimmy,' he said, looking like an errant urchin who has been roundly chastised. 'The social workers said the kids weren't getting any kind of education here at all, that their progress had already been badly affected.'

'You going to do it?' I asked, holding out my mug as he went back to the tap.

'Don't see as I've much choice,' he said. 'But the way I see it, I'll send 'em for a short while until all this fuss dies down, then I'll take 'em out again and no one'll be the wiser.'

'And that was the only thing they asked you to do?'

'The kids have to be sent for a medical. A checkup, like. They said they thought they weren't gettin' enough to eat. Jaysus, every time I look at one of the little feckers they're stuffin' somethin' in their gobs.'

We drank on in silence. I watched him with my peripheral vision. He seemed to be coiled, as if the slightest thing could send him into either hysterical laughter or bilious rage. I decided to poke the sleeping bear with a stick to see what might happen.

'How has all this been on you, Tom?'

'What?'

'How are you doing? Man to man, no one here but us two guys. How are you coping with all this stress? Your brother is trying to take your home away, the thing you have worked your whole life for. Now social services are suggesting that your parenting skills leave something to be desired. That's enough to shake anyone's foundations.'

Tom swallowed and looked at his bulging stomach.

'I'm a'righ',' he said in a little voice.

'Really?' I asked disbelievingly. 'I don't know many people who would be. Aren't you even a little stressed?'

Tom shrugged, sniffing all of a sudden. He coughed and turned his face away.

'You've had your drinks now,' he said in a voice that sounded as if it were coming from under a blanket. 'You can go on. Dora will fix you something to eat. Tell her I said.'

I said nothing more, just put the mug back and left the room. I didn't go looking for Dora, just started to walk the ragged roadway back towards the road, and once I reached it rang for a taxi to meet me. I had learned all I needed to know – things were beginning to move.

26

I rang the school mid afternoon and asked George Taylor if I could meet him for a few minutes. He said he could spare ten at half past five, so I made sure to be punctual.

'What can I do for you, Shane?'

'I'm not sure if you can really do anything, but I think I have to bring something to your attention.'

'All right. I'm listening.'

'Do you know a gentleman named Jeff McKinney?'

'Of course. He's in the storeroom as we speak organizing some photographic equipment for tonight's group.'

'He works for you?'

'Just some odd jobs. He was a student here and I just . . . I took an interest in him, I suppose.'

'He's not doing a course then?'

'Here?'

'Yes.'

'No. Not that I know of.'

'He told me he was.'

'I daresay you misunderstood. What of Jeff, anyway?'

'Well, you know how I called him a gentleman?'

'Of course.'

'It seems he's not.'

Taylor gave me a funny look, and I launched into a summary of what Carla and Jessie had told me, without mentioning their names. The principal sat and listened without motion or comment until I was finished.

'And of course you have the phone messages with his number attached.'

'No. I may be able to get them, but I'm not sure the girls in question want to be involved to that degree.'

'So the complainants are not willing to come forward either?'

'They're kind of embarrassed.'

George Taylor shook his head sadly.

'You will forgive me for thinking that what we have here is a vulnerable man being victimized.'

'Not a disturbed man hiding behind his disability?'

'Shane, there is nothing I can do. Give me evidence and I will act, I promise you. But there is not a lot I can do with Chinese whispers and hearsay.'

I knew he was right. I thanked him and went to meet Gladys.

As my meeting with George Taylor was so short, I got to class an hour and fifteen minutes early, armed with the materials I needed for that night's session as well as one or two things for Gladys's literacy assessment. I had some suspicions as to what her problems might be, but wanted to hear her reading and also get a look at some written work before I jumped to any conclusions. I turned on the lights, set up my computer so I could simply begin when the rest of the group arrived and then laid out the work I intended to do with Gladys.

Then I sat down to wait.

And I waited some more.

Gladys never turned up for any classes on time. I had noticed this, and it was one of the things that made me wonder about her literacy issues – there are certain learning difficulties that carry particular contiguous symptoms, one of which is complete lack of organizational skills. This knowledge did not make her dogged refusal to reach destinations at the carefully prearranged times any less irritating – I blithely thought of half a dozen things I would rather be doing than sitting in an empty classroom long before I needed to be. But I shoved these thoughts aside and settled back with another volume of *Preacher* to await Gladys's arrival.

At 6.15, a quarter of an hour late, Gladys arrived.

'Sorry, Shane,' she said, looking genuinely apologetic. 'I left the house in time but got . . . waylaid.'

'Sit down,' I said, shaking my head. 'We have less time now than I would have liked, so I don't want to waste any of it. Have a look at this.'

I pushed a magazine across the table. It was one of those celebrity gossip rags, with lots of photographs. I opened it on to a page recounting the latest exploits of the pop singer Britney Spears. Her behaviour didn't really divert me much, but it seemed to be of consuming interest to a lot of other people and I gambled that Gladys would be one of these.

'Have a go at the story I've circled,' I said.

'You want me to read it?'

'Please. I'd like to hear how well you get on.'

The thing I liked about the magazine was that a lot of the information needed to successfully read the Britney article was already commonly known, or could be gleaned from the photographs that surrounded the columns. Gladys began haltingly, but soon picked up speed. The vocabulary in the piece was very simple, and though she stumbled over a few of the words – celebrity, bipolar, antisocial all caused her to pause – she did not seem deterred.

When she finished, I could tell the experience itself had done her good.

'You did well,' I said. 'I would hardly call someone who can read a full magazine article illiterate. I can see that there are one or two problems, but they're nothing we can't get over. Let's up the ante a bit. Here's a book. It's a novel, so I'd like you to read from here to here,' I showed her where I had marked the page.

I'd chosen a section from the American writer James Patterson. His books are compulsive, fast-paced and contain short, punchy chapters. The book I had chosen, *Cross*, utilized few lengthy words, and I thought Gladys would do well with it. To my surprise, though, she struggled. Looking over her shoulder, the words that were tripping her were words she had read with ease in the magazine. Finally I cut in.

'Do you know what's happening?' I asked.

'I'm fucking up big style,' she said.

'You're allowing yourself to be intimidated because it's a book. You read all these words with no problems five minutes ago. The only difference is that now they are contained between the covers of a book.'

'I don't know,' she said.

'Try again.'

She did a lot better, though she was still very jumpy. Finally, I dictated a short piece, no more than three sentences, and got her to write it down. When she was finished I looked at her work, and knew immediately that my suspicions had been correct. But there was no time to discuss them, as I could already hear the first of Gladys's peers coming up the corridor.

'Can you grab a drink after class and I'll chat to you about this,' I said, tapping the page.

'Okay,' she said. 'I can do that.'

The evening flew by – we were talking about different

cultures and how the childcare worker must be aware of things like diet, language and religious festivals, not to mention being generally inclusive in terms of imagery on posters and in books as well as in toys and equipment. We had a good old discussion, and before I knew it the group were filing out. Gladys hung about until they were gone, and then led me to a little pub at the top of the town which was mostly frequented by old men playing cards.

'So,' Gladys said, looking really nervous. 'Can I be fixed?'

'You don't need fixing,' I said. 'There are three things I want to say to you. Number one, and this is as important as all the others, you have to start believing that you *can* do things. Just because some old asshole told you once that you can't or won't succeed doesn't make it so. Stop being scared of books. A word is the same whether it is in a book or a magazine or a comic. Understand?'

'Yes.'

'I think you have a condition called dyslexia. See in the piece you wrote for me? You've written several words back to front, or you've got the letters pointing the wrong way around. You haven't done it a lot and judging by how well you can read, I think it's a very mild case. I'd like to show what you've done to an educational psychologist, just to have it confirmed.'

'Uh – okay. If you say so.'

'I also wonder if you might have a condition called dyspraxia. It causes people to be disorganized and to lose concentration. This could be why you used to get in trouble at school. Did you seem to be very clumsy then?'

'I was always tripping over stuff.'

'Yeah. That's probably it. Again, we'd have to have you properly assessed, but I think we've nailed it.'

'Oh my God. Dyslexia. I don't know what to think.'

'Don't get bogged down by the label. You're still you.'

'And you think I can read well?'

'You read well tonight.'

I held out the James Patterson book.

'I offered you a book to read a few months ago and you ran out of the room as if I'd pulled a gun on you. I'm asking if you'd like to borrow this one. You don't have to read it all. But maybe try a few chapters and tell me what you think.'

She took it and looked at the cover.

'I'll give it a go,' she said. 'What's it about?'

'A psychologist trying to catch a serial killer.'

'Bit of light bedtime reading then,' she said.

'Would you prefer something on flower arranging?'

She put the book in her bag.

'Hell no!'

27

I was engrossed in an article on Garshaigh's recreational park, which had been built right after Ireland received independence from Britain in 1922, when the phone on my desk rang.

'Yeah. Shane Dunphy.'

'Shane, this is Nathalie Lassiter at the primary school. I'd be obliged if you could call over today at some point that's convenient.'

I looked at my watch. I was on a deadline for the piece I was writing, but it was close to finished. Another hour would do it.

'What are you doing for lunch?'

'That would be fine. Can you come to the school? This is a rather sensitive matter.'

'I'll be there. See you soon.' And we hung up.

She met me at the door, looking worried.

'I have checked out your credentials, Shane,' she said. 'I hope you don't mind.'

'It's been happening a lot lately,' I said. 'Have I done something to cause you concern?'

'No. I want to hire you.'

'I have a job, Nathalie. And I'm not qualified to teach at primary level.'

'No, you misunderstand me. I want you to act as a consultant. A rather serious child protection concern has arisen and I regret to say that, while the school does have child protection policies, they are somewhat out of date.'

I sat down. Like before, she had a tray containing coffee and, this time, sandwiches, on her desk. I poured for us both.

'I'd be happy to help out,' I said. 'Payment is not really necessary.'

'I'd prefer to keep this very much by the book,' Nathalie said. 'If you were a parent I could put you on some committee or other, use your expertise that way. But you're not, and there are barriers to your sitting on any of our committees, anyway.'

'Oh?'

'Let me begin at the start of all this. Please, eat while I talk. I know I'm taking up your lunch break.'

I took a sandwich, which I could tell had been sent over from the café where Carla worked. It suited me fine.

'I don't know if you're aware, but the Blaney children – Emma and Dom – have been sent here as of the start of this week. To minimize stress, I have placed them in the correct class groupings for their age, but for a couple of hours a day a remedial teacher is working with them. They are really delightful children, Shane. Very sweet, very loyal, but as I am sure you would expect there have been some behavioural issues. Dom has gotten into quite a few fights, and has hurt one boy very badly. And, God help me, Emma is a climber. Her teacher came in to the class yesterday to find her – literally – swinging from the light fitting. I have no idea how she got up there.'

'Emma is quite the acrobat,' I agreed.

'Their academic levels – for every single subject – are

171

remarkably low. Neither child can read at all. Dom can count to ten, but beyond that is a new frontier for him. It is as if they never received any schooling at all. I must draw the conclusion that they didn't.'

'I know that social services are aware of all these things,' I said. 'You will probably be asked to attend what is called a multi-agency case conference within twelve months of the kids starting at the school, but that will be to share general information, and get a sense of how other professionals are experiencing the kids.'

'That's not the only problem, though.'

'I see.'

'The best thing for me to do is to call in Kyla. She's the remedial teacher I mentioned.'

Nathalie picked up the phone, dialled a number, waited.

'Kyla, would you mind joining us now, please?'

Moments later a short mousy woman with thick glasses, wearing a tweed skirt and a brown cardigan over a blue polo-necked top, came in.

'Kyla, this is the gentleman I told you about. You can speak freely in front of him.'

The little woman sat on a chair beside mine.

'Mr Dunphy.'

'Shane, please.'

'Shane, I have been teaching now for close to twenty years, and I am not prone to exaggeration. I have worked with difficult children for most of that time, and in terms of language and general conduct, the Blaney kids are nowhere near as bad as some I have had in my care. But I am morally bound to share with you exactly what they said.'

'I'm listening,' I said. 'Please use the language they did, and don't try and make it palatable or polite – I'm used to this sort of thing. I have a fairly high tolerance threshold.'

Kyla took a deep breath, as if in her head she was approaching the distasteful task at a run.

'We were doing some role-play – some drama. I like to get the kids to act out stories after we've read them; it helps to imprint the structure of the books into the children's memory.'

'Good idea,' I said.

'Thank you. We had just read *Jack and the Beanstalk*, and Emma was reciting the giant's chant, you know, about how the giant will grind Jack's bones to make his bread. Suddenly she stopped, looked at me, and asked what did the rhyme mean.'

'She's a bright girl,' I said. 'But I expect the language puzzled her.'

'Quite. Well, I told her that the giant, being a big bad monster, planned to *eat* Jack if he caught him.'

'How'd that go down?' I asked, already knowing in my heart what the answer was going to be.

'Emma nodded, as if she had expected as much. Then she said: "Like when Bad Daddy makes me eat his pinkie." '

'His finger?' I said.

'No. She showed me on a doll exactly what she meant by the term. And that was just the beginning. Once she started talking, it was as if she couldn't stop. Dom sat impassively at first, looking as if he did not approve of this confession, but after five minutes or so, he started to add his voice to the choir, too. I have written it all down, Shane. You can read it at your leisure. Suffice it to say that those children have been forced to endure every type of human debasement. And not just with the father. Jim, the eldest boy, has, according to Emma and Dom, been replacing his father in the marital bed when Tom is away overnight.'

I nodded. Part of me had expected this, but a larger part had hoped it wouldn't come to pass. Neglect and beatings were quite bad enough. This just kicked it all to another level.

'You say you have everything recorded – written down?'

'Yes. I signed and dated it, also.'

'Nathalie, you need to write up your side of things too. Your impressions of the children. Do you still have any details of Jim's time here?'

'I already dug that out.'

'We need to take this to social services. Do you want me to act on your behalf?'

'No, I'll do it,' Nathalie said. 'Could you just read over the reports and see if we've got all the detail they'll need? I can give you this room for as long as you need.'

I thanked her and took the bundle of paper.

As the two women were leaving me to my work, I called Nathalie back.

'You mentioned an obstacle to my coming on to one of your committees, to cement my role,' I said. 'What did you mean?'

She waved the question off.

'Doesn't matter now. It was just your not having a child at school here. They like school business, particularly sensitive stuff, kept within the families, you know?'

'Okay,' I said and thought no more of it for a day or two.

28

It was a testament to Sid's professionalism that a case conference was called rapidly. As the school's designated consultant, and, I believed, out of respect to my former role as a child protection worker, I was invited to attend.

The meeting was held in the local community centre, not far from the newspaper's offices. Around the table was Sid and his boss Josephine Welch, Doctor James Sounding, the family doctor, Nathalie and Kyla, George Taylor, who had Jim and Winnie at his school, and myself.

Josephine, for whom I had retained no fondness since our last encounter, chaired the gathering. She began by giving a brief family history, mentioning Jim's earlier brush with social services and the by now famous court case. She outlined the children's ages and then handed the baton to Sid, who gave a concise report on his and Josephine's visit to the house.

'It was clear that the children were dirty, hungry and very nervous. It did not take long to establish that they were not receiving any educational training, despite their mother's insistence that they were, and I could see patterns of bruising on both Dom and Jim.'

Doctor Sounding was up next. The doctor admitted that he

had been the family's GP for his entire career, but had really only seen Dora just before each of the children's births. He had been asked to carry out a medical examination on each child by social services, and in most of the children's cases this was the first time he had encountered them. The doctor stated that each child was physically small, probably due to malnutrition. He spoke of scarring and bruising on all of the siblings, these marks being indicative of regular and severe beatings. He had ordered X-rays to be carried out, as he suspected that there were old bone breaks that had healed over time.

'Due to the information that has come to light since then,' he nodded at Kyla, 'I will also be recommending a full examination by a sexual abuse assessment team, and screening for sexually transmitted infections. These children have been appallingly badly treated, and I, personally, feel deeply ashamed that I did not take a greater interest in their welfare. All the signs were there; we simply chose to ignore them because it made our lives easier.'

George Taylor had little to add.

'Jim and Winnie are academically very far behind. Jim has a cursory understanding of the most basic literacy and numeracy, but at the level of a child in the junior cycle of primary school. He is progressing quickly, however. I think the lack of practice is mostly to blame. He will never be an A student, but I think he may even pass the Leaving Certificate with the right support. He is a quiet, dour young man, but there has been no real trouble. Winnie, however, is very problematic. She is profoundly illiterate and innumerate, and she exhibits signs of serious emotional trauma. She is verbally and physically abusive to children and staff alike – I frankly am uncertain as to whether my school can absorb her. She may need a special placement.'

Josephine said nothing, but made a note of this.

'Any disclosures, Mr Taylor?'

'None. The children barely communicate at all.'

I was asked then to relay my part in the whole business, and I recounted our picnic at which I saw the bruises on Dom and the art-work exercise when Bad Daddy was first introduced to me.

'And I believe that Bad Daddy shows up in your story too,' Josephine invited the staff from the primary school to take the floor.

Nathalie and Kyla took turns in recounting their experiences with Emma and Dom, complete with a full recounting of the younger children's disclosures. There were many winces and looks of extreme discomfort from those hearing these for the first time.

'The children have continued to assert that all this is real and did happen,' Kyla concluded, 'and new stories are emerging every day – usually variations on what you have heard, but I believe they indicate a long-term, regular and concerted campaign of terror and abuse, from *both* parents, although I believe Dora's role seems to be centred around her relationship with Jim. Emma and Dom do not see her as abusive – they describe her as something of a nonentity in fact.'

When everyone had spoken, Josephine looked around at the group.

'It seems clear to me that there is only one course of action left open to us,' she said. 'However, I'd like the consensus of the group.'

'Tom and Dora are not fit to care for those children,' Doctor Sounding said firmly. 'I cannot stand by and allow those babies to be abused on a continual basis any longer. I say we seek a care order. Today if possible.'

'I agree,' Kyla said.

'In my experience a voluntary care order is always more

desirable,' I said. 'But yes, I think it clear that home is not safe for the Blaney kids.'

'Are we being a bit drastic?' Nathalie asked.

All heads in the room turned to her. This was an unexpected turn of events.

'You have driven this enquiry,' Josephine said. 'Are you changing your mind?'

'No, no,' Nathalie said. 'I just wonder if the kids need to be taken into care. They're so close, and in care they would be separated.'

'We have thought about that,' Sid said evenly. 'We are seeking a placement that would accommodate all four children.'

'Are we adding pain to the suffering they've already experienced?' Nathalie asked again.

'There is no way to do this that is easy and painless,' Sid said. 'We are trying to perform emergency surgery without the benefit of anaesthetic. It will hurt like hell while being done, but the long-term benefits should make it worthwhile.'

'I don't know,' Nathalie said. 'I'm not happy about all of this. I think we're playing God with this family's life.'

I watched her. Something wasn't right. This woman had been adamant about interceding. Why was she now so against it? She wouldn't meet my eyes, and she ran to her car when the meeting broke with no firm decision made.

The girl paddled just on the waterline, delicately dipping her big toe into the water. I noticed that she never went any further than that, as if it was an unspoken rule.

'Do you ever go swimming?' I asked her.

'No. We don' never get in de water.'

'Why not?'

'My daddy say it bad for us to get in. Him can't swim. None of us swim neider.'

'It's fun, being able to,' I said. 'You have this beautiful beach. It's a pity not to get the most out of it.'

'Dad don't never come down here. Mam don't. They scared, I think.'

'But you're not,' I said.

'No. I not scared.'

'You should never get in when you're on your own,' I said, 'But maybe we could arrange to get you some lessons.'

She tiptoed along some more.

'Dad says they monsters in the sea. He says they getcha if you go too deep.'

'You wouldn't be going deep,' I said. 'Up to your waist, maybe.'

'You ever see a sea monster?'

I laughed.

'No.'

'I not see a *sea* monster,' she said. 'I seen a monster though.'
'You did?'
'Yeah,' the girl said, 'Monsters is real, all right.'
I had a feeling she was being totally truthful.

29

I awoke from a dream I could not remember that night. The moon was shining through a crack in my bedroom window, casting a beam of white light across the room like a laser, settling in a spot in the door. I felt uneasy, anxious, and sat up, looking for Millie, who I saw was standing staring at the door as if there was something beyond it. I got up and pulled on a T-shirt. She looked back at me, whined, and then returned her attention to the door.

The hallway was lit up like it was day, the moon's radiance unimpeded by curtains. Millie walked rapidly ahead of me and stopped in the entrance to the living room. I came up behind her, and saw what had aroused her attention.

Lonnie was standing with his back to me, looking out the window at the street beyond. Except I somehow knew he was not really looking at the night-time thoroughfare – he was seeing things far beyond it. Things I could not, maybe never would, perceive.

Millie trotted over to him and he held out his hand for her to sniff, then rested it on her head.

'I did what you wanted,' I said.

'Did you?' he asked, not looking at me.

'I went to social services. I made the referral. The kids are going into care . . . probably.'

Lonnie turned his focus back on the street.

'Right over there, where the drapery shop is now. That building used to be the county home,' he said.

'I didn't know that,' I said.

'You know what the county home was, don't you?'

'It was similar to a poor house,' I said. 'An institution for people in trouble. Residential care for the community.'

'You make it sound very pleasant,' he said.

'I doubt that it was,' I said. 'I haven't researched it much.'

'The point about the county home was that it had little to do with the needs of the people who ended up living there. It was mostly about putting them somewhere where the general population didn't have to look at them.'

'I think a lot of care is like that,' I said.

'Make sure that is not what happens to the Blaneys,' he said, and his voice was hard and commanding.

'Hey,' I said, annoyed. 'You tell me to go to social services or else. Now you're telling me to make sure the kids *aren't* put in care if that isn't the best thing – I mean, their parents are starving them and abusing them and not sending them to school.'

I threw my hands up in exasperation. 'I tell you what, Lonnie – *you* tell me what's best for them, 'cause I'm getting pissed off being shoved around from Billy to Jack!'

'What's best for them is that which will make them happiest and cause them the least pain,' Lonnie said, and then I was standing looking at the window, and he was not there. Millie sniffed about the carpet and whined at me for a moment, but I had no idea if I had dreamed the whole thing.

30

Sid Doran dropped by the office to tell me the Blaney children would be coming in to the local health centre for some more tests, so I thought I might call over and see how they were coping.

There was no sign of Tom when I got there, just Dora looking piqued and worried. The children didn't look great either. Jim was pale as a ghost, deep rings under his eyes as if he had not been sleeping. Winnie had a deep gash across her forehead as if she had been hit with something sharp. Dom was sitting on the floor in the corner rocking, his arms about his knees. And little Emma was wandering about the room crying, darting at unseen things in corners and starting at shadows.

'They're trying to take my babies away from me,' Dora said, the electric buzz of hysteria very plain in her voice. 'I can't believe this is happening. They can't take the children! They just can't!'

'Has anyone told you the kids are going to be taken?' I asked her, making a grab for Emma, catching her and putting her on my knee.

'They don't need to,' she said. 'Social workers – that's all they ever want. I know. I know how these things work.'

Emma made a hiccoughing sound and I hugged her tight. She was so little, so tiny, yet had experienced so much. I wanted to take her away and read her a story, or sing her some songs. The unhappiness and depression were heavy in that room. It was no place for a child.

I wondered how often I had caused families to sit in rooms just like this, heaping more blackness on their already stooped shoulders.

'Doctor Sounding has organized for the children to have some tests done, that's all,' I said, trying to soothe her. 'No one is getting taken away today.'

'Maybe not today.' she said. 'But soon. Could be any time, now. They'll come and we won't be able to stop them.'

I stayed while each child went in and came out looking shocked and even more upset. I thought of what Lonnie had said the previous night: was this really making things better? What had I set loose on these children? Was the cure, in this case, worse than the disease itself? There had been a time when I was resolute about such things. Not now. Watching all this happen from the sidelines, I was coming to believe that everything I had stood for was wrong.

The tests that were being carried out that day were to establish whether or not the children had – in theory – engaged in inappropriate sexual behaviour. This involved checking if the girls' hymens had been broken and if there had been any overt stretching of the rectal opening in the boys. Swabs would be taken to see if there were any residual traces of semen. No matter what way you looked at it, the tests were undignified and invasive.

I watched the faces of each child as they emerged from the surgery and felt as if I had molested them myself. Emma would not look at anyone when she came out. She just curled into a ball on one of the chairs.

I told Dora I would call out to the house soon, and left.

When I got outside, Gerry Blaney was sitting on the bonnet of my Austin.

'1981 Austin Allegro, Series 3 Saloon,' he said, patting the bonnet. 'Original fire orange finish – you have resisted the urge to paint go faster stripes on her – I commend your restraint. Hydraulic suspension, 1.31 engine capacity, has a round wheel rather than the square, quartic variety they tried to pilot. You take good care of her.'

'I like her,' I said. 'She treats me well if I return the favour.'

'How much do you want for her?'

'She's not for sale,' I said.

'Stop messing about. How much?'

'You're not listening,' I said. 'The car is not for sale. Not for any amount of money.'

'Can I take her for a drive?'

'No,' I said, opening the door and getting behind the wheel.

Gerry came around and sort of leaned over (he didn't need to bend down) to speak to me.

'Those kids are in a right state, aren't they?'

I didn't answer. What he said was true, but I was not going to encourage him if I could help it. I didn't like him or trust him.

'You know Tom and me don't see eye to eye, but I hate to see those little kids and their mother in such a mess. I know you have some experience in this area – sure hasn't the school taken you on as some kind of consultant? Use your influence. Put this thing right.'

'I couldn't even if I wanted to, Gerry,' I said. 'As soon as social services came on board it was out of my hands, or anyone else's. The kids are the state's responsibility now.'

Gerry grinned and laughed. It was not a nice sound.

'Eight hundred years ago, Garshaigh was part of a kingdom

governed by Richard de Burgh. Henry III had given him the title of King of Connaught, but some of his lands were also in Munster, hence Garshaigh falling under his remit. So, he could have asserted his will over everyone in this town, and I'm sure at times he might even have done that. However, in the main, he left local decisions to be made by his local representatives.'

'The Ponse de Blaneys,' I guessed.

'Precisely,' he said. 'Back then local problems were dealt with locally. Small towns have long memories. The old ways die hard, here. Maybe you should think about that before you go sticking your nose in where it isn't needed or wanted.'

I leaned out so my face was very close to his.

'I'm just a journalist for a local paper,' I said. 'Sending a few yokels out to frighten me is probably not going to get you in that much trouble. But, see, there are social workers involved now, and gardai. Taking a shot at them, now that will bring all kinds of hassle down on you. So if I were you, I'd keep *your* nose out. In case someone comes along and knocks it off.'

I started the engine and pressed the accelerator so he had to pull back quickly or get dragged beside the car. It was a childish move, but I enjoyed it tremendously.

31

The story was getting legs, and the legs were pumping furiously.

As the court date for the hearing on the will came closer, the national media got wind of the land war between the two powerful men: the eccentric farmer and his successful, entrepreneur brother. Robert Chaplin was asked to pen pieces for several national newspapers, and we received so many requests for radio interviews that we had to take turns fielding them. Robert even had to drive to Dublin to make some TV appearances, and the national station came to Garshaigh to do a report – Robert was asked to act as advisor on locations and to suggest some other local people for interviews.

My boss seemed to think all his Christmases had come at once. For a man who rarely smiled and generally looked as if he had just been given a stinging slap across the face, he strode about with a permanent smile plastered across his chops. He replaced his threadbare, shiny pinstripe with a new suit (still pinstripe, but cleaner) and even started talking to me again, which alleviated some of the tension about the office.

The child protection issues had been leaked by someone,

but there was absolutely nothing any of us could say, for the simple reason that the children had not, as yet, been taken into care, and neither parent had been prosecuted or even charged with anything. Our line when asked about it was that we were unaware of any outstanding child protection issues in relation to the Blaney family, and could therefore not comment. Next question.

The fact was that the blend of big business, small-town politics and family drama, combined with a frisson of child abuse, created a story that was irresistible.

'This will run and run, Shane my lad,' Chaplin said gleefully.

He even allowed me to write a few very short columns on some peripheral elements of the case. I knew this was my editor being unspeakably generous, but the truth was, I didn't really care either way. I still felt guilty about what had happened and was worried about how the children were faring. I knew that their imminent removal from their home was pretty much a done deal, but I could not get little Emma's face out of my head. I wanted to go out and see them, but was sure I would end up making things worse if I did.

'You step back now and let the professionals do their job,' Chaplin said when I told him what I was thinking. 'God knows, they'll do whatever they want anyway. It's not like your opinion counts for anything.'

The fact that he was right did not help one bit.

I was at the local farmers' market one Saturday morning in the middle of all this kerfuffle. As I settled into the house I was renting my mind began to drift more towards making time for the things I liked to do, and one of these was cooking. Since my arrival in Garshaigh I had been living on sandwiches, coffee and the occasional bowl of soup. I'd just had no interest in anything more elaborate. However, as spring came in and the sun began to warm the earth I started to feel the urge to tamper with recipes again.

The farmers' market seemed a good place to start.

Millie and I wandered among the stalls, sampling this, smelling that and generally having a grand old time. I had the ingredients for a fish stew with saffron rice that I had been craving, and was sitting on a bench drinking a glass of freshly squeezed apple juice from a nearby stall when I felt a mild thud against the base of my seat. Turning, I came face to face with Jeff McKinney. He had piloted his chair so that it collided directly with the side of the bench. I wondered if he thought this would upset or discommode me. It didn't. It just struck me as odd.

But then, Jeff McKinney struck me as an extremely odd person.

Neither of us said a word for a moment, simply eyeballing one another. Then Millie started to growl, which is extremely uncharacteristic of her – I placed my hand on her neck immediately to soothe her, but could still feel her shuddering. Her eyes were fixed on McKinney, her tail thrashing back and forth, her teeth bared.

'What's wrong with your dog?' McKinney asked, though there was no alarm in his voice.

'I don't know,' I said. 'Maybe she smells a rat somewhere hereabouts.'

He took the jibe in his stride.

'You've been talking about me behind my back,' he said.

'Have I?' I retorted. 'What about?'

'Don't act all innocent,' he said. 'Mr Taylor asked me about some personal messages I've been sending. How did he know about those messages?'

'Maybe the people you sent them to weren't happy with their content,' I suggested.

'Or maybe someone who wasn't supposed to read them went running to the headmaster to squeal.'

Millie had settled a bit, so I stopped holding her collar and just stroked her head. She was still staring at Jeff, but I didn't think she was likely to try and pounce on him.

'Look, what are you trying to say?' I said, getting bored with the verbal evasion. 'Did I get some complaints about messages you had sent to some of my students? Yes I did. Did I speak to Mr Taylor about them? Yes again. I'm sure you're annoyed about it, but that really isn't my concern. Make sure the person on the other end is open to that kind of interaction before you go sending explicit messages. It's a basic courtesy.'

McKinney's manner changed abruptly. He darted around the bench and made a grab at me. I slid sideways and Millie again growled, louder now, and lunged forward. I caught her just in time, or she would have ended up in my aggressor's lap.

'You stay out of my affairs!' McKinney said. 'I'm warning you now – I will make things very difficult for you if you keep annoying me. I promise you that.'

In a final act of defiance, he rolled off – right over my foot, which I thought was a nice touch.

'That is one weird little guy,' I said to Millie as we watched him trundle away.

She made a sort of snort of agreement, which I appreciated.

32

I left the school three nights later with Jessie, to loan her a book I thought was in the car.

'I think this'll give you a better picture of what I'm talking about,' I explained. 'It doesn't have a lot of text, but the photos chart the first five years of Maria Montessori's first school after the Vatican took an interest in her. The pictures are really remarkable.'

We rounded the corner to the school's small car park, and I walked straight into someone – or rather that was what I thought had happened until I received a blow right into my solar plexus. I folded over like a sheet of paper and went down.

If that is Jeff McKinney again, I thought, *he has really been working out.*

'No smart comments today, paper boy?'

I rolled over and saw that my assailant was the one I had come to think of as the leader of the local goons – the group who had tried to run Tom and his family off their land, and had also asked me to stop visiting them. By twisting about I could see the other three gathered about my car. I tried to tell Jessie to run, but I couldn't get any air into my lungs to fuel speech. Lip-reading the words as I mouthed them, though, the girl got my meaning and took off.

'So, we need to have a little chat,' the man said, picking me up under my armpits and dragging me over to his cohorts. 'God, you're a heavy bastard, aren't you?'

'He is weighty with his own self-importance,' the broad, squat one said.

The others laughed at that. I didn't think it was very funny, but kept my opinion to myself. I didn't think my input would be welcome.

They propped me up against the car and, when they were sure I wasn't going to fall over again, the ringleader said: 'You've been asked nicely. We've given you ample opportunities to do the right thing. I mean, I don't think anyone could say that we've been anything other than patient with you. But no, you had to be a stubborn class of a fella and make life difficult for yourself.'

'It's a character flaw,' I said hoarsely. 'I'm working through it with my therapist.'

'There you go again with the smart commentary,' he said. 'Do you realize that you are leaving us no choice but to inflict quite a serious amount of pain upon you?'

'What do you want?' I asked, my voice starting to return to its usual timbre.

'Okay, okay. You wish to establish a dialogue. That's a good start. Well, since you ask, our goals have altered somewhat since our last exchange. Previously, we wanted you to keep away from the Blaney household. Now we would add to that the wish that you do all in your power to prevent social services from taking the Blaney children into care.'

'I already told Gerry that I have no influence at all with child services. You've got the wrong guy.'

'That,' my captor said, seizing my chin in his hand and shaking my head from side to side, 'is a very defeatist attitude. I mean, we know you were at the case conference, and that you get regular updates from the social worker on the case, a Mr Doran. That would suggest at least a *degree* of influence. Maybe we need to teach you some self-belief. Baz, come over here and give Mr Dunphy some motivational instruction.'

Baz never got to move, because the sound of an engine starting caused everyone to spin around. Standing at the corner, dressed in his grey suit (tie tucked safely into his shirt front), with a set of goggles covering his eyes and holding his trusty blade strimmer, was George Taylor principal extraordinary. He revved the power tool a couple of times, then allowed it to go into a gentle idle.

'Get off my grounds,' he said, and I sensed each of the four shrink slightly – his voice held in it not a trace of doubt. This was a man who expected utterly to be obeyed.

'Now, you run along Mr Taylor,' the ring leader said. 'You don't want to get involved in this.'

George laughed brusquely and began to walk towards them, revving at every step.

'You are in my school,' he said, 'so I am already involved. You are threatening violence upon one of my staff team, a person who it is my duty to support unequivocally. Now . . .'

He switched off the strimmer and tossed it aside, pulling the goggles off and putting them on a windowsill out of the way.

'There are two of us and four of you. Do you wish to throw down fisticuffs?'

Baz was starting to look very unsure of himself.

'Look – you got no part in this.'

Taylor poked him hard in the chest with his index finger.

'You brought me into it when you walked through that gate over there,' he said, and he was angry now. His voice and body language seethed with it. 'How do you want to do it? One on one until we knock one of yours down, and then the other steps in, or just all pile in together?'

The four looked very bothered. They had not expected anything like this.

'Oh, and Shane,' Taylor said, incidentally. 'Try not to let the side down, will you? There is a security camera up there,' he pointed to a pole just behind us, 'over there,' – when I looked I could see one set on the eave of the building to our left – 'and over there.' This time he pointed to a spot on the roof of a building across the street, but right opposite us. 'When I look back at this with the police, I want to be able to hold my head up in the knowledge that we gave these yobs as good as we got.'

'Fuck this, I'm out of here,' Baz said. 'I'm not fightin' that guy. He's off his feckin' head.'

'Me either,' the squat fat one said.

'Well, that evens it up,' Taylor smiled, advancing on the leader. 'Queensbury rules?'

Before he could take up his stance, the final two ran for the gate.

'Cowards,' Taylor said, then turned to me. 'Are you all right?'

'I got sucker punched,' I said, rubbing my abdomen. 'I'll live.'

'What did they want?'

'For me to try and prevent the Blaney kids being taken into care.'

Taylor nodded.

'Well then I am doubly sorry we did not have the opportunity to teach them a thing or two.'

'Mr Taylor,' I said, slapping him on the back. 'You really are crazy.'

'And don't you forget it,' he said, picking up his strimmer.

33

I was out at the Blaney house when they came to take the kids.

I had tried to keep away, but two things drew me back: number one, every time I put any food into my mouth, I wondered when Emma or Dom had eaten last, and what their repast might have been. This began to be something of an obsession: I would try to imagine the circumstance – where would the children be? Would they have purloined some food or would their mother or father have given them some? Would it be some crusty bread, or a piece of fruit, or perhaps some cured meat as I had been given for lunch my first time there? Would there be enough to go around or would someone be left hungry? Would it be nothing but a tantalizing taste, just enough to torment the starved palate, or a gut-stretching feast?

I also needed to see Emma. Her terrible anguish that day at the medical centre haunted me. Of all the kids, I had bonded with her the most, and I found the idea of her feeling so upset, so helpless, to be quite unbearable. I was fully aware that any pain I was experiencing was nothing compared to what the children were going through, but that didn't help.

I decided to bite the bullet and drive out.

When I arrived, I found the children had been forbidden

even to leave the house. Tom was certain they would be snatched if caught out of doors, so he reasoned that it was best to keep them inside. He was down in his war room, and had no interest in talking to me.

'Dora has taken to her bed,' he said. 'Stay for a bit if you want. I have work to do.'

I sat with Jim, Winnie, Dom and Emma in the living area. The kids seemed to eschew the furniture: we all sat cross-legged on the floor in a loose circle.

'I brought you these,' I said, handing out ham salad rolls.

They were taken without question and attacked immediately.

'So what's been going on since I saw you last?'

'Mammy sick,' said Emma through a mouthful of food.

'Is she?' I asked. 'What's wrong with her?'

'She gotta pain in her belly,' Dom said. 'She won't get out've her bed. Bad Daddy shouted at her, and hitted her, but it don't make no diff'rence.'

'Will you stop talkin' about Bad Daddy,' Jim snapped. 'That's what has us in trouble in the first place!'

'You think you're in trouble?' I asked. 'Why do you think that?'

'Good Daddy told us some men might come and put us in jail,' Emma said. 'We has to keep an eye out for them, 'cause if they come they gonna take us and bring us some place far away from Mammy and Daddy and our house. I don' wanna go t' prison. I wouldn' like that, bein' in with all them bad people.'

'But you're not in trouble,' I said. 'No one wants to put you in prison.'

'No, we are in trouble,' Dom said. 'Why did that man hurt us that day in the health centre? He did awful bad things to us – things like Bad Daddy does. Good Daddy said that people done heard about Bad Daddy, and they thinks we done

196

somethin' to make him bad like that, and we has to be punished for it.'

'But you didn't make your dad do anything,' I said. 'He did bad things because he's a little bit ill in his head. You are not, and will never be, to blame for that.'

'We shouldna telled nobody though,' Emma said, leaning her head against my arm. 'That's what has all this trouble comin'. We telled and now they want to lock us away. Thas what happens. One of the kids in school tole me.'

'That kid is wrong,' I said.

Sometimes fate is perverse and enjoys dramatic effect.

At that precise moment there was a loud knock on the door. Jim got up to answer it. I heard muffled muttering from down the hallway, a muttering that gradually built to an angry exchange, and which ended with Jim screaming:

'Dad! Daddy – they've come! They've come to take us away!'

It took me a second to register the information. The children looked at me open-mouthed. I grabbed them to me in a fierce hug and said: 'It'll be all right – you're going to be scared and your dad is going to be very angry, but I will stay with you – I promise.'

None of them answered, and I didn't have time to wait – I had to get to Jim.

I got up and ran towards the shouting, praying that whatever was about to happen would be controlled and as gentle as possible. When I got to the door, I saw that was not to be. The front yard was full of cars – it looked as if every social worker in the Garshaigh region, as well as most of the police, had come out for the removal. Jim had thrown himself at Sid Doran, who was nursing a bruised jaw. The youngster was being restrained by two flak-jacketed police officers. He was shouting and spitting, trying desperately to get loose and finish what he had started. As I watched, he lashed his head back and butted one of the guards full in the nose. The hurt man snarled and used his forearm to clout Jim across the face.

'You treat that boy gently!' Sid shouted, but I was already across the yard and had shoved the man back. He loosed his grip on the boy, but his partner still held firm.

'Keep it together!' I said through clenched teeth. 'The kids are not the criminals here.'

The guard was squaring up to me, his eyes streaming and a trickle of blood coming from his right nostril.

'Who the fuck are you to tell me what to do?' he snarled, reaching for his baton.

'This man is with me,' Sid shouted, getting in between us. 'He is part of the team. Now let's get this done as fast and as painlessly as we can. Get the boy in the van, okay?'

Jim was carried kicking and screaming towards the paddy wagon that was parked near the front door.

'Where are the adults?' Sid asked me.

'Inside. Dora is in bed, Tom is in his office.'

'Show me,' he said, and my heart sank.

'We need to be very careful with the children.' I said. 'Tom has their heads all messed up about what's going on.'

'I'll tell you what,' Sid said as we walked down the hall, 'you take the kids to the van and stay with them, and let me deal with Tom. If we can minimize the trauma of all this, it would be best for everyone.'

'Do you have a care order?' I asked.

'Not yet. I'm going to try and get Tom to sign a voluntary one, but if he won't do it we'll go the Section 12 route.'

Section 12 of the Child Care Act allowed social services and the gardai to remove children from their home without a warrant, if there is reason to believe the child is at serious and immediate risk of harm. It is not a popular course of action, but in some cases is essential.

When we got to the living area the three remaining children were sitting in a tight cluster, their arms around each other.

'Kids, you remember Sid,' I said, trying to sound upbeat.

'Daddy says he is a bad man,' Emma said. 'Why you with him?'

'He wants to talk to your daddy,' I said.

Right then there was a roar and Tom crashed into the room, throwing furniture aside as if it was made of cardboard.

'Bad Daddy!' Winnie cried, and covered her head with her hands.

I ran to the children and tried to get them to stand up, come with me, but they were tangled with one another and would not move. Out of the corner of my eye I saw Sid fleeing the way he had come, Tom in hot pursuit.

'Come on, you lot,' I said. 'I need to talk to you and you're not helping.'

'We ain't goin',' Emma said. 'You s'posed to be our friend. Why you bein' mean t'us?'

'I *am* your friend,' I said, feeling like the world's biggest liar. 'I am trying to help you right now, even though it doesn't look much like it.'

'You should run too,' Dom said, peering over his shoulder. 'Bad Daddy gonna come back soon, and he will not be happy to see you here.'

That thought had occurred to me, but I didn't know what else to do other than try to coax the children outside.

'Why don't you come with me and we can talk about exactly what's going to happen?' I said.

'We goin' away?' Emma asked, tears welling in her blue eyes. ' 'Way to jail?'

'Not to jail, I already said that,' I said gently. 'To another home. I don't know yet, but I'll ask as soon as we go outside, and we can find out all about it.'

'Will you stay with us?' Winnie asked, crying now too.

'Of course I will,' I said, the tears streaming down my cheeks too. 'As long as you want.'

The three kids unwrapped themselves from one another and, hand in hand, we all walked slowly down the hall. I could hear the muffled shouting of Tom, and the sound of Josephine Welch giving orders, but other than that all seemed peaceful. When we got outside we were greeted by the sight of Tom splayed out on the ground with three guards sitting on him. When he saw me leading the children out, he renewed his efforts, shouting at me for all he was worth.

'You fucking good-for-nothing *traitor*! I let you into my home! I broke bread with you, you faithless *bastard*!'

'He is gonna hurt you *bad* when he gets loose,' Dom said.

I walked the children past their father and opened the door of the paddy wagon. Jim lurched out at me, but when he saw his brother and sisters he settled back down.

'Would you like me to see if I can have the radio turned on?' I asked.

All four heads nodded in unison.

I was walking around to the front of the van to do just that when Josephine's mobile rang. I paid little heed – I would have expected that she was liaising with the venue we were about to bring the children to.

'Can we pipe the radio through to the back?' I asked the guard in the front of the van. 'The kids like music.'

The man nodded and switched on the stereo. The vehicle filled with the sound of loud Top 40 dance music.

'Okay everyone,' Josephine suddenly said, raising her hands and calling for our attention. 'There has been a change of plan. Stand down, let Mr Blaney loose and bring his children out.'

I snapped around.

'What are you talking about?' I asked. 'You can't do this!'

'I haven't done anything,' Josephine barked at me. 'Someone has brought a court injunction against us. We cannot take the children into care. Let them go.'

The men restraining Tom let him go and, in huge lurching steps he rushed to the paddy wagon and wrenched open the door, taking the four children into his beefy embrace.

'I don't fucking believe this,' I said.

Sid Doran stood a little apart from it all, watching without expression.

'I better never see your face again,' Tom hissed at me.

I turned on my heel and left him to it. I wanted to throw up.

34

'What the fuck happened?' I shouted at Sid Doran.

We were in his office, which was marginally bigger than my broom cupboard.

'As you heard, someone applied for – and got – an injunction. An injunction is a legal writ preventing us taking these children into care.'

'Why would anyone want to do that?' I asked, realizing as the words came out of my mouth that I already knew the answer. 'Gerry Blaney. The evil little prick.'

'Your assessment of him is most certainly correct,' said Sid, who was sitting back with his feet up on his desk. He was wearing brown suede Vans. They looked comfortable. 'But in this case he is not the culprit.'

'That doesn't mean he isn't behind it in some way,' I said.

'I don't know. Maybe you can dig around and find some kind of connection.'

'You're killing me with the suspense, Sid. Who did it?'

'Father Eli Loughrey.'

'*Father* Eli Loughrey?'

'The same.'

'It makes no sense,' I said, pacing the tiny room. 'The

Blaneys don't even go to Mass. Why would the church step in?'

'Well, it's actually more complicated than just the church jumping in to save the day. Loughrey is retired – he's like ninety-eight or something. His main business these days is heading up the local chapter of an organization called The Knights of the Crucified Emperor. They're an extreme faction within the Catholic Church. Believed to be very rich and very powerful.'

'I've never heard of them.'

'Most people haven't. They're one of those behind-the-scenes groups that have allegedly been pulling the strings of politicians, big businessmen and even the media for years. It's probably mostly bullshit – they're meant to be in there with the Illuminati. I've met Loughrey. He's an old toad who thinks he should still be top dog.'

'Doesn't help us.'

'No.'

'So what can we do?'

'The injunction means that, not only can we not take the Blaney kids into care on the issues currently on the table, but neither can we pursue other issues to achieve the same end. It basically supersedes all other childcare legislation.'

I gawped at that.

'That's ridiculous. You can't go to court to stop the law applying to your children!'

'It seems you can,' Sid said. 'Look, you don't know me, but I get the sense we share some qualities. I don't take stuff like this lightly. I'm going to fight it.'

'Good for you,' I said. 'How can I help?'

'I'll let you know when I've decided what to do. Right now, I still can't work out why Loughrey and his Knights want to stop us helping the Blaney brood.'

I sat and thought about it. I had never heard Tom, Dora or any of the children make any reference to God or Jesus or spirituality. The letter Tom had shown me was written in the style of an Old Testament prophet, but I didn't recall any actual allusion to religion in it. In fact, if I remembered correctly, the text gave me the sense that old man Blaney saw his family and the heritage of his ancestors as the only religion that held any sway over him. Suddenly the answer popped into my head.

'It *is* Gerry Blaney,' I said. 'Just like we had initially thought – he's behind it.'

Sid waited for me to elaborate. He never seemed to waste words if he didn't have to. I liked that in him.

'When I came here first, Robert, my editor, told me that Gerry was involved in every organization there is locally. He mentioned the Masons and the school board – and he said that he had his finger in every pie in town. Makes sense that he would be in these Crucified Knights if they have a local chapter.'

'Okay, I'll agree your logic holds up,' Sid said. 'But how does the knowledge help us?'

'It makes us feel accomplished and a little less embarrassed,' I offered.

'That is better than nothing,' Sid agreed.

Neither of us came up with anything else, so it had to do.

The girl was crying. I tried to console her, but she was utterly bereft.

'What's wrong, sweetie?' I asked, stroking her hair and trying to get her to look at me.

'Go away,' she sobbed. 'You leave me now.'

'Why do you want me to leave you? You're upset and I want to help you.'

'You can't help me. Nobody can help me now.'

'I'm your friend, sweetheart. I'm not going anywhere.'

She buried her face in her hands and cried with renewed pain and bitterness.

'Just tell me why you're crying,' I said, trying a different tack. 'Tell me that, and I'll go.'

'Daddy says you want to take me away from him and from this here place! He says you lyin' to me. You not my friend at all!'

I said nothing for a time. Daddy was right, about my intentions at least.

'I am your friend, darling,' I said. 'No matter what anyone says, I am your friend.'

'Not if you lie to me,' the girl said through her tears. 'I can' abide people who lie. You tell me a lie an' I'll *never never* fergive you.'

I wanted to tell her that I would never do such a thing, but I knew even that was bending the truth. I let her cry, sitting beside her in her hideout in the copse, stroking her blonde hair and wondering how to make it all right.

35

Days blended into one another.

Garshaigh is a small place, and everywhere I went the people I encountered had a view on the case. Despite the fact that not a single word had been printed about the attempt to place the Blaney children in care, someone had been talking and the entire story (exaggerated beyond belief in some versions) had made the rounds, and the fact that I had been on the scene when it all went down had not escaped notice. The part I had played – and those I had sided with – was also the focus of much conjecture, but I limited my responses to a smile and a wink, accompanied by a 'now if I told you, I'd have to kill you.' It didn't make my interrogators happy, but it gave them something else to talk about, namely what a bastard that new journalist with the *News* was – *he has ideas about himself, that one does.*

I shouldn't have been surprised by the fact that most of the people I spoke to – in truth, the vast majority – had made up their minds in favour of the Blaney parents.

'Tom and his people have been farmin' that land since Celtic times,' Benjy Dulsk, another big farmer from just outside the town, informed me. I had been hoping for a quiet pint in the pub where I had chatted to Gladys about her reading.

'The number of Garshaigh people that family has employed down through the years would probably fall somewhere in the region of several thousand,' Benjy said. 'They say that, in penal times, it was Jehoshaphat Garshaigh who offered the local priest a hiding place in the old ash grove, and let him say Mass by that shelf of rock there – the old folks here still call it the Mass rock.'

I realized as he spoke that this was where the children had taken me for our picnic the day they had drawn their pictures and first told me about Bad Daddy. I shivered at the thought.

'In 1916 Samson Blaney, Tom's grandfather, organized a contingency of men to travel to Dublin to participate in the offensive in the GPO. It is even said, and I, for one, believe it to be the case, that Samson Blaney had a part in the drafting of the Declaration of Independence that was read from the steps that day. The Blaneys are part of the history of this town and the country itself. You don't disrespect people like that by telling them they don't know how to raise their own children.'

'Even if those children are obviously suffering?' I asked moderately.

'Now who are we to be the judges of that?' Benjy asked, and I decided to keep my mouth shut – nothing I said was going to change this man's mind.

The following day I was due to cover the day's district court proceedings. In Ireland, the district court hears minor criminal cases, smaller civil matters (it cannot award damages over €6,348) and a jury does not oversee any of its dealings. For the readers of the *Western News*, the district court was a source of great gossip and entertainment. For many of our regular subscribers the reports we printed on the district court proceedings were the first items they looked for every week. Who had been caught driving a little too fast? Whose son had been arrested for being drunk and disorderly? Which couple had been cautioned by a garda for rowing publicly and causing a disturbance?

I could understand the attraction. Small towns are like goldfish bowls – not an awful lot happened, no matter how hard or long you watched, so you learned to glean excitement from the small things.

Covering the court was a long day. You had to remain focused and make a point of jotting down each and every detail accurately because, as Chaplin pointed out to me on my first day on the job, the individuals who appeared before our judge as miscreants were also some of the most litigious people you were likely to meet.

'Get it right the first time and we won't have to be printing withdrawals and apologies,' he said, 'or end up making our own news by finding ourselves in court.'

On the day in question the judge had called a break for lunch, and I was packing my notebooks, pens and other odds and ends into my bag when I heard my name being called.

'Hey. Dunphy. You there.'

I looked up to see a middle-aged, besuited man with thinning blond hair. I recognized him as Keith Dignam, a solicitor who had been representing a young man who was up due to a lengthy backlog of traffic offences.

'Yes?' I said, assuming that I must have spelt his name wrong at some point in the past.

'Lay off the Blaneys, all right?'

I looked around to see if there was anyone else he could possibly be talking to.

'I wasn't aware that I was laying *on* them,' I said.

'They are a great family and they deserve our respect, not to be labelled as child abusers and pariahs.'

'And who has labelled them any of those things?'

'Your newspaper—'

'—has printed nothing about any child protection issues whatsoever.'

'Well its stance on the dispute over the will—'

'—has simply reported fact. Even if we did come down on one side or the other, we'd still be siding with a Blaney, so I don't really get your problem.'

'It is a matter of *tone*,' he said sagely. 'You treat the thing as if it were a circus sideshow rather than a matter of human dignity.'

'I'll take your comments on board and report them to my editor,' I said, getting up.

If I stayed around I would have said something I might have regretted.

Two days later I was at an auction of a group of derelict farm buildings that adjoined an old mill near the town boundaries. While quite a crowd turned out, there was little real competition for the properties, and Trapper Healy, a grossly obese, sweaty man who wore suits meant for somebody of a much slimmer frame, ended up being the only serious bidder. He was the most successful property developer and real-estate agent in town, and he hoovered the entire catalogue up as if the buildings were so many grains of sand. I had never even been introduced to Healy before, and I would never in a million years have thought that my humble comings and goings would have registered on his radar, but as soon as the gavel had been pounded the final time, he was making a beeline for me.

'You,' Healy said, no friendliness in his voice at all. 'You're the child welfare lad.'

'I'm a journalist, Mr Healy,' I said. 'I write for the *Western News*. That's why I'm here today. Congratulations on your acquisitions, by the way.'

'Yeah, yeah, right. Now, I want to have a word with you

about this Blaney affair. You don't want to go runnin' about, and you nothin' but a blow-in, from *Dublin*, probably, getting people all upset and annoyed. It's not good for morale. Jesus, I mean to say, any other time I'd've had a small bit of a fight to get these sheds, but you saw it today – no one had any heart for it.'

'You think that I am causing a downturn in the local economy?'

'What you're doin' t' poor Tom Blaney is affectin' everyone.'

'If you have something to say about the children's well-being, I suggest you talk to Sid Doran or Josephine Welch at the offices of child services. I know you don't believe me, but I have no authority and no remit here at all. I am purely a writer who became something of an . . . I don't know . . . an acquaintance of the family in recent weeks.'

'You don't fool me, you beardy feckin' upstart,' Healy hissed, putting a hand on my chest and gripping my shirt. 'We've had you checked out. I know you were a child welfare busy-body for a lot of years, and I know you have a history of interfering in all sorts of things you should've kept well clear of.'

'Really?' I said, looking confused. 'Me? Here I was all this time thinking I was a by-the-book child protection worker. I mean, I've never been in trouble, never had any disciplinary action against me, I've always had a good relationship with the gardai – am I missing something, Mr Healy? Do fill me in if I've skimmed over something important.'

He gripped my shirt tighter and in a reflex action I shoved him away.

'You are hurting my town,' Healy said, breathing hard. 'I won't stand for it.'

'Sit down then,' I said. 'And for God's sake buy some clothes that actually fit you.'

Feeling as if I may have sunk even below his level of

discourse, yet not feeling one bit guilty about it, I skulked back to the office.

I shouldn't have been annoyed by the altercation, but I was. I sat at my desk two hours later, long after Chaplin had gone home, glowering at my computer screen, which contained little more than a flashing cursor and the words: *Auction Sellout*. I was proud of the headline. I thought it was short, snappy and controversial. Now if only I could come up with something to put below it. Like an article.

I heard a foot on the stair and thought it must be Chaplin back, but then realized the tread was too light. A knock on the door followed.

'Come in,' I called.

It was Rachel, one of the students from my night class.

'Hey,' I said. 'Have you got something exciting for me to put in my column this week?'

She smiled bashfully and sat down opposite me. She was a pleasant-looking girl with brown hair and a petite frame. She was dressed in the uniform of a checkout girl. I knew she worked in the local supermarket.

'Shane, I think I'm in trouble,' she said, and I saw she was about to cry.

'Take a deep breath and tell me about it,' I said, going over to the cooler and getting her a glass of water. I grabbed the box of tissues from Chaplin's desk and handed it to her.

'I . . . I don't know what to say,' she said. 'I mean, I haven't even got a boyfriend. I wish I could tell you what I did to have made this happen.'

'Make what happen, honey?' I asked.

She fumbled in her bag and took out her mobile phone. I felt my heart sink.

The message this time was much, much worse. The previous

ones were of the 'this is what I'd like to do if I ever got hold
of you' variety, and were obscene but fairly pedestrian in
their content. This one was nasty. It was cruel and angry and
very, very threatening. I checked the number. It was from
McKinney's phone.

'Do you have any suspicion as to who sent you this?' I asked
her.

She shook her head.

'You didn't give your number to anyone new?'

'No.'

'You're sure?'

'I'm certain.'

She stopped for a moment, as if a thought had occurred to
her.

'I lost my phone last week. In college.'

I looked up.

'Where did you lose it?'

'I noticed it was missing when we were in the computer
room. Remember you were showing us how to use those data-
base sites?'

'Yes, of course. Can you remember if you had it when you
went in to the computer lab?'

'No, but I must have.'

'Why do you say that?'

'Because I looked and looked and couldn't find it. I was
sure it was gone for good. Then when I was going home, I met
that guy in the wheelchair – you know, Jeff – well he had it.
He said he found it under the desk I'd been working at. I was
so pleased he'd found it. All my numbers and a load of other
stuff is on it.'

I smiled, though I wasn't happy.

'When did the texts begin? The bad ones?'

'I got the first one the next afternoon.'

'Okay, Rachel. You were right to come to me. Here's what I want you to do . . .'

And I told her a plan I had been formulating. She agreed to help me.

36

'Erik Erikson was a Danish-American psychologist,' I said, a series of photos of the man being projected on to the board. 'He dedicated his life to developing a set of what he called "psychosocial stages" of development, which took the ideas of Freud, some of which we looked at a few weeks ago, and turned them into something most people find a lot more useful.'

'He looks kinda like a more serious Einstein,' Breda said.

'Mmm. I believe he was a happy man with quite a sense of humour,' I said. 'He was certainly popular with his students. But he was always searching for somewhere to belong, somewhere to call home. Just like Freud and so many of the other theorists we've discussed, Erikson was Jewish. But he looked like the stereotypical Viking – very tall, very broad, with yellow blond hair. So at Jewish Sunday school he was bullied for looking like Eric the Viking. At mainstream school they bullied him for being a Jew. As soon as he finished school, he ran away, travelling around Europe and farther afield, trying to find himself, as so many young people, both before and after him, have done.'

'Did he ever find it?' Rachel asked.

'What?' I asked. 'Himself?'

'No,' Rachel laughed. 'A home.'

I looked at the final picture of the great psychologist, looking into the camera with a determined, if slightly tense, expression.

'I don't know,' I said. 'I like to think he did. He was very happily married, and he spent a lot of time with the First Nation Peoples when he came to America, and he always wrote that he was very comfortable with them.'

'Maybe he did then,' Tim said. 'If you think about it, when you lose something, it's often in the last place you look.'

'That is a very profound observation, Tim,' I said.

There was, at that point, a knock on the door and George Taylor stuck his head in.

'Hello everyone,' he said, smiling at the class.

'Hullo Mr Taylor,' they responded as one.

'Shane, I have someone looking to have a quick word. Can you spare a few minutes?'

I brought up a slide that outlined Erikson's stages.

'Get into groups of three or four,' I said. 'Look at the names of the stages, see how they are all "something vs something else" – Erikson said that each stage involved a conflict. So, the first stage, which is the first year of life, is called *Trust vs Mistrust*. The second year of life is *Autonomy vs Guilt*.'

'What does "autonomy" mean?' Maggie asked.

'Who has a dictionary app on their phone?' I asked, looking about the group.

No response.

'Who can get one for free within twenty seconds?'

About twenty hands went up.

'If you don't understand any of the words, look them up. I want you to go through the stages, all of which are posted on the board there, and discuss why you think Erikson gave them those names. What did he mean by identifying each stage by those conflicts? What did he think was going on in the person's head? I'll be as quick as I can, and then I expect you to share your insights.'

Taylor said goodbye to the class and then led me towards his office.

'I would have asked your visitor to wait until the break, but he assures me this is an urgent matter that simply cannot wait.'

'Yeah? Who is it?'

'Father Peter Ahern.'

'Don't know him.'

'He is the bishop's personal assistant. His right-hand man.'

'It's probably something to do with the paper,' I said. 'I'm sorry, Mr Taylor, I'll get rid of him as fast as I can.'

George patted me on the shoulder as we reached the door of the office.

'The bishop is our patron,' he said. 'Take as long as you need. If you're not out in half an hour, I can tell your group to take an early tea break. I doubt they will be too upset at the prospect.'

I gave him a thumbs up and went in.

The room was in darkness except for one lamp on George Taylor's desk. Sitting in the principal's seat, his hands forming a steeple in front of him, was a dark-haired man of perhaps thirty-eight years. He wore the black clothes and white collar of a priest, and had a pleasant, genial face.

'Shane, thank you for taking the time to see me,' he said, standing when I came in. 'My name is Peter. We haven't met.'

I shook his hand as we sat. It was all very friendly.

'Mr Taylor has filled me in on who you are, and urged me to give you as much time as you require,' I said. 'So – what can I do for you?'

'I'm here to ask you, in your capacity as a writer for the

biggest-selling local newspaper in the region, to do me – and his Lordship, Bishop Kantwell – a favour.'

'What kind of favour?' I asked.

'The kind that will be remembered. The kind that can earn you favours in return.'

'I'm a man of simple tastes, Father, and of few needs. I assume the favour involves writing something for the paper. That is my job, so, if you have an item worth publishing, I'll facilitate that, no problem, no reward necessary. If the bishop has something he wants to say, the newspaper is hardly going to turn him down, now is it?'

'You are a pragmatic man, I see,' Father Ahern said.

'I like to think so.'

'Very well. Let us not beat about the bush any further. Are you interested in history, Mr Dunphy?'

'Yes.'

'You are aware, then, of the great struggle Roman Catholicism has faced over the centuries in Ireland. The church has been persecuted by a succession of British monarchs – priests burnt at the stake or skewered like pigs, property stolen, manuscripts burned, valuable artefacts taken. Catholics were viewed as being little more than criminals, members of a dangerous cult.'

'What does this have to do with anything, Father?' I asked. 'With the greatest of respect, I grew up in an Ireland with an obscenely wealthy Church whose authority was only questioned when it was brought to light – after years of collusion – that that power was being unspeakably abused.'

'I am surprised to find that you are a bigot, Mr Dunphy,' Father Ahern said, his voice pregnant with anger.

'No, I'm not a bigot,' I said. 'I just don't think playing the poor mouth is very seemly in these times. And I assure you, our readers won't go for it.'

'Whether you like it or not, Mr Dunphy, the Church has been through some real challenges in the past, as it is going through a period of difficulty now. And throughout those times there have been people who have helped us – come to our aid, despite personal cost – and those who have turned away and disowned us.'

'To each their own,' I said. 'You cannot blame a population who has been abused and lied to for being angry. If you want people to accede to your moral authority, you need to demonstrate that you have some.'

'You are not from Garshaigh, are you, Mr Dunphy?'

'No. But I bet you know that.'

'You grew up in Wexford. It was terrible, what happened in Ferns – a real hotbed of clerical abuse. Don't think for a moment that I support abusers. Those men who did those terrible things deserved to be prosecuted. The Holy Father saw they were divested of their powers as priests and rightly so. I know you were part of the investigations. I admire that.'

'I appreciate your candour,' I said. 'Father, this is getting us nowhere. I really don't have an axe to grind against the Church – I have made my peace with it, and have good friends who are involved with religious orders. I don't know you, and I don't know the bishop. Tell me what you need, and let's see if I can help or not.'

'Very well,' Father Ahern smiled, opening his hands expansively. 'Let's do that. Allow me to cut to the chase, as they say. Over many, many years, the Blaney family has done innumerable acts of service and charity for Mother Church. In fact, it is claimed that Siegfried Ponse de Blaney brought back a chalice from the Holy Land that was said to have been owned by Paul the Apostle. Siegfried gave this relic to the Bishop of Garshaigh in 1249. Because of this selfless act, the bishop made him a Knight of the Church, and that title has been handed down, from father to son, ever since. It is not simply a conceit, Mr Dunphy. It means that the family are *under our protection*.'

'Father, I have a great deal of affection for the Blaneys,' I said, suddenly feeling very tired. 'I seem to be doing nothing lately but talking about this family, and trust me, I have done *a lot* of soul searching and I do feel that I have done my level best to help them. But you have to understand, I am not a social worker, I am not employed by child services – there is not a damn thing I can contribute to whatever campaign you lot are trying to mount!'

'Do you know that the injunction is being challenged by the social work department?'

'I did not know that,' I said. 'But I'm not surprised.'

'The Blaneys have been dragged through the mud for long enough. His Lordship wants it stopped. A *lot* of people locally want it stopped. You will begin a series of articles celebrating the history of the Blaney family. I know Robert Chaplin is in the midst of writing a book on them, I'm sure he will give you the bare bones of their accomplishments – that should suffice. I know you cannot address the challenge outright, but we can sway public – and even judicial – opinion in other ways.'

I sighed and stood up.

'I have to get back to my class,' I said. 'Thanks for dropping in.'

'You'll do it?' Father Ahern asked, looking pleased.

'No.'

The priest looked as if he might pitch backwards in shock.

'You do not understand – if this travesty continues, the fall-out will be terrible!'

'I do understand. There is no way to do this where the children will not suffer. But I also know that if they stay where they are, their suffering will be worse.'

I opened the door.

'You are aware of the bishop's role in the school here?'

I closed the door and walked back to the desk.

'I am aware of that, Father,' I said. 'If you want to try and have me sacked, you go ahead. Who knows, maybe you'll do it, too. But let me tell you this – you won't stop those children being helped. You managed to slow up the process a bit, but that's just a blip. Go on.' I slammed my hand down on the desk, making him jump. 'Do your worst. If I have to lose a part-time job to make sure Winnie sleeps safely at night – well, it's a small price to pay.'

I walked out and didn't look back this time.

37

I needed some space and to taste the wind so instead of walking Millie through the town, as I usually did, I took the road that led to the beach. But I turned off to the left before reaching the sand, heading into the woods.

I let Millie off her lead and she scouted ahead, virtually invisible in the darkness with her black coat. I kept track of her running ahead of me by the ID disc on her collar jingling against the metal tag with her microchip details engraved on it. She loved the woods – for my dog they were a cornucopia of scents and sensations. Her entire being seemed to become alert. Even in the dark I could feel the electricity emanating from her as she barrelled about, sniffing here, peeing there, rooting in the undergrowth someplace else.

I had brought a torch, but only used it where I was genuinely worried I was going to hurt myself. The cover of night felt good. I was starting to develop the sense that Garshaigh – not just the people, but the personality of the town itself – was closing in on me like an enormous black-gloved hand. I acknowledged that I was being just a little bit paranoid, but the regularity with which people were popping out of the woodwork pointing the finger of blame at me over the Blaney case – or outright assaulting me – was becoming more than slightly irritating.

As a professional child protection worker, I was used to people trying to sway my opinion one way or the other – and not just the families and friends of the children on my case books. It was quite usual for the people on my team to disagree on the management of cases, and there could be a fair amount of healthy and occasionally heated debate.

The difference in those instances was that I was part of a large, government-run organization (or a wealthy voluntary one) and had the weight of the entire system behind me, along with all the other groups I regularly worked with – I had been friends with many members of the police force when I worked in the city, and had a wide network of colleagues and associates to call on in moments of doubt.

In Garshaigh I was not exactly isolated, but I was certainly the odd man out in the Blaney case. And I knew that was why I was being targeted. The lead man on the case was Sid Doran, but he was a social worker with the Irish health services, and therefore not a man to send a bunch of thugs after. He had a legislative role and was a state employee, so interfering in any way with his legal challenge of the injunction could result in criminal charges being brought against the interfering party.

Josephine Welch was the social work team leader and senior social worker in the Garshaigh area. As team leader she co-ordinated the case, but in reality had little to do with the Blaney family and had more of an administrative role in the whole thing. I had heard that she took her position *very* seriously and was a hard woman. I'd had a little taste of that myself on my first meeting with her. She was not an easy person to influence one way or the other.

From what I could tell, Nathalie Lassiter at the school had already been got to. By the time we had the case conference she was already saying she was not supporting a move into care for the Blaney children – a complete turnaround from what she had told me at previous meetings.

I wondered how Doctor Sounding was faring – had he been approached by anyone?

The trees broke in front of me, and I knew I was on the Blaney's land. Flat fields stretched towards the horizon, and the sea opened up to my left. Millie took off at a sprint, running in great loops, enjoying this rare chance to do what nature had designed her for. I watched her for a few minutes, then followed a natural path through the field. Every now and again I could hear the whirring alarm call of a snipe. Once a fox crossed my path, totally disinterested in me. Millie gave her distant cousin a disdainful glance, and continued with her foraging.

I found the ash grove with little difficulty, but had to use the torch to find my way through it. The path was criss-crossed with roots and brambles, and I had to pick my way daintily through them. Moments later I was out in the hollow and there, looming above me like a claw reaching for heaven, was the Mass rock. Millie looked at it and whined, then trotted back over to me. Using the torch I found a flat area, approximately where Emma, Dom and Winnie had sat with me.

'This is an ancient place,' a voice said and, slowly, Lonnie emerged from the trees.

'Isn't everywhere ancient, if you really think about it?' I asked.

'Most places have layers of existence piled one on top of the other. Not here. This place is much as it was when people first walked on it.'

'Well the church is claiming it as its own,' I said. 'Welcome to the Blaney family Mass rock.'

'They prayed to many gods here, over the millennia,' Lonnie said. 'No faith had a specific claim.'

'You've gotten very learned since taking up ghost duties,' I said.

'I'm trying to strike a Yoda-like presence.'

'It's working. I like it.'

'Thanks.'

We sat listening to the trees for a while.

'It's worse than ever down at the house,' Lonnie said.

'Really?'

'It's all coming apart for them. If something is not done, there will be a great tragedy.'

'It's out of my hands, Lonnie,' I said. 'It's all down to Sid and social services.'

'You can't affect the outcome of the case,' Lonnie said, 'but that doesn't mean you can't be there for the children.'

'How? Tom has threatened to kill me if I come near the place. This is as close as I want to risk getting – at night, when they're all asleep.'

'Tom is so far from reality right now, he doesn't know what's going on. The kids come here a lot. If you were to come out early and wait for them – with some food, perhaps? It would mean a lot.'

'You think?'

'They're in a bad way, Shane.'

I scratched Millie behind the ears. She was lying between the two of us, content.

'Okay. I'll see what I can do.'

'I know you will.'

Nearby a barn owl shrieked as it careened through the sky, a pale ghost on the wind.

'Lonnie,' I asked.

'Yes, Shane?'

'I'm completely off my head, aren't I? I mean, I've really gone off the deep end.'

'Very probably,' he said. 'But then, who knows? Sanity is just a state of mind.'

'That is utterly meaningless,' I said, but he was already gone, absorbed by the darkness.

'You alieve in God?' the girl asked me.

'I don't know,' I said. 'That's a very hard question.'

'My dad says there bes a God and angels an' all.'

'Does he?'

'He says we gots ta pray to them. That be like talkin', on'y nobody talks back to ya.'

'Do you like praying?'

'No. It's stupid. I think it be a right waste of time.'

'Some people get a lot of comfort from it,' I said. 'They really feel God is listening.'

'You pray?'

I marvelled at the complexity of the conversations I had with this child. She knew how to put me on the spot.

'Sometimes, yes.'

'You pray t' God?'

'No. I talk to my mam, sometimes, and I have a . . . a very good friend who died, and I talk to him, sometimes, too. Actually, I talk to him a lot.'

The girl sucked her teeth and thought about that.

'They ever talk back to ya?'

'Sometimes it's like they do. Especially my friend.'

'If somebody talked back when I prayed, I might do it more.'

'What do you say?'

'To God?'

'Yeah.'

'Mostly I ask for stuff.'

'What kind of stuff?'

'Stuff I can't have.'

'Toys and things like that?'

'No. Not like that.'

'What then?'

'I ask him to make things better.'

I put my hand on her shoulder.

'That's a good prayer,' I said.

'*He* musn't think so, 'cause He still hasn't made it happen.'

38

I met Sid Doran for lunch in the restaurant at The Grapevine the next day. I hadn't been back to the hotel much since moving out, and even when I had lived there I hadn't felt brave enough to eat in the restaurant.

I perused the menu as I waited for the social worker to arrive. They had prawn cocktail. They had Caesar salad. They had garlic mushrooms. The soup of the day (I had been told as I sat down) was cream of vegetable. Probably out of a packet. There was a steak sandwich – hard to mess that up. Unless you cooked the steak to the point of leather. I wasn't making much headway.

Jeff McKinney rolled in the door of the restaurant, saw me and scowled. He scooted over.

'What are you doing here?'

'I would have thought it was obvious that I was having lunch,' I said.

'I could have you thrown out,' McKinney said. 'I think I will.'

'Do you know who I'm having lunch with?' I asked.

'Why should I care? One of the little whores from your class, I'd guess.'

'I'm meeting a social worker.'

He narrowed his eyes.

'Why?'

'Maybe I'm going to tell him about the foul message one of my students showed me the other day – a message that came from your phone.'

McKinney went pale for a millisecond, then regained his composure.

'I don't know what you're talking about,' he said.

He rolled away a little, then turned rapidly and said, in a voice that was almost a shout:

'You're a sick fuck, you are!'

Then he was gone, off somewhere among the myriad service corridors of the old hotel.

Sid came in, looked around for me, waved and came over.

'Do you eat here a lot?' I asked as he put his pack down on the empty chair beside him.

'No, I've never eaten here at all,' he said.

'So why did you ask to meet here then?'

Sid thought for a moment.

'It's near where you work. I thought it would be convenient.'

I smiled and nodded – convenient, if uncomfortable – but then, how was he to know?

'Well, that is thoughtful of you.'

I asked the waitress if I could just have a toasted ham and cheese sandwich, mustard on the side, and a bowl of soup (I reckoned I would brave it). Sid got the steak sandwich.

'So how has the campaign been going?' I asked when she went to get our food.

'Well, as you know, I have launched a challenge against the injunction.'

'Do we have a time frame for that?'

'I wish it were so simple,' Sid said.

The waitress returned, bringing Sid a pot of tea and me a cup of coffee. I took a sip. It was hot.

'Tell me about the complications.'

'Well, according to the rules of discovery, our lawyer has to be given all the paperwork and information from their side. So we now have the full picture on how the injunction got through, despite all the evidence we had that the Blaneys are not only unfit, but are actively abusive.'

'And?'

'Well, as we already knew, the process was paid for by the Church through the offices of the Knights of the Crucified Emperor. But in reality, they're just a front.'

'For whom?'

'The injunction very probably would never have gotten through by itself. It was accompanied by a – well, a petition, really. It goes on for a bit, so I'll paraphrase it for you: it posits that Tom and Dora Blaney are exemplary parents, who are utterly devoted to their children, all of whom are glowing examples of well-rounded, articulate, athletic youth. It suggests that the decision to cast aside the trappings of modern twenty-first-century life is just one example of how Tom and Dora have made sacrifices to ensure their children's safe, unpolluted upbringing, and that they should be looked upon as shining examples of how children *should* be parented. Finally, it puts forward that certain members of the town have made it their business to try and tarnish the reputation of this great family, and that it is the duty of the court to prevent such a travesty occurring.'

'Sounds like quite a piece of writing,' I said, laughing.

'This letter is signed by Father Loughrey, but is then co-signed by twenty other names. Most are business people – farmers, accountants, lawyers, local politicians. They wouldn't worry me – you could fairly easily show that they have never even seen Tom Blaney with his children. No, the name that bothers me is that of Nathalie Lassiter.'

'Nathalie signed it?'

'She did. It looks like she was the last one to do so, but her name is on the page and that is very damaging to our case.'

'She was wavering when we met last,' I said. 'Wouldn't have taken much to turn her.'

The food arrived. We had some. The ham and cheese wasn't bad. The soup was awful, and that it was hot was still the kindest thing I could say about the coffee.

'How's your steak sandwich?' I asked as Sid chewed.

'Well in fairness, they don't specify which part of the cow they're using,' Sid said, around a mouthful.

We worked on in silence.

'So what are we really talking about here?' I said when my sandwich was gone and I'd had as much of the soup as I could cope with. 'Why would a bunch of professional, generally decent people go out of their way to stop some children being taken from a situation that is harmful to them?'

'There's a long tradition hereabouts of not interfering with what goes on behind the walls of a family home,' Sid said, giving up on his own meal and leaving it half finished. 'People don't like to be seen as informers or squealers.'

'I know what you mean,' I said, 'but this isn't like that. It's not that these guys are being *asked* to get involved by telling us anything about how the Blaneys are with their children. They are choosing to throw their tuppence ha'penny worth in. They're *putting themselves* into the picture.'

'I have a policy when it comes to anything involving business people,' Sid said.

'Do tell.'

'You can apply it to almost anything involving the Blaneys, too,' he said. 'When in doubt, follow the money trail.'

'That had occurred to me, too,' I said.

'I haven't worked out how it all fits yet,' Sid said, 'but it's the only thing that makes any sense.'

We talked about it for another hour, and still couldn't get the pieces of the puzzle to come together.

But I knew we were getting close.

39

The court date for the civil dispute surrounding old man Blaney's will finally arrived. The notoriety and celebrity nature of the case meant that the court was full. I sat beside Robert Chaplin, my boss virtually trembling with excitement – moments like this were defining moments in his life. Tom and Dora, wearing exactly the same clothes they were dressed in the last time I saw them, sat looking decidedly shop-worn and rumpled, front and left. Beside Tom was Keith Dignam, the solicitor who had tried to work his charms on me. I laughed to myself – the dots were beginning to join up.

Gerry, escorted by a blonde woman thirty years his junior and a foot-and-a-half taller, sat front and right, a snappy young lawyer I did not know accompanying him.

Judge Xavier Grundy (willow thin, rheumy eyed and tight lipped) oversaw proceedings. There was, at first, a lot of boring evidence from friends and associates on both sides, who were either falling over themselves to say that, yes, they were in absolutely no doubt at all that Jacob Blaney was in the best psychiatric health imaginable, or no, that he was a raving lunatic who ate his own faeces and believed he was receiving messages from an alien race. Neither group was wholly plausible or completely unbelievable. If anything, they all looked like they were being paid to be there.

Then Gerry's side called their secret weapon.

'Would Doctor Roger Brunswick take the stand, please,' Gerry's lawyer, whose name was Steven Horton, said.

Doctor Brunswick was as diminutive as Gerry, with a head of thick greying curls and an impressive pair of beer-bottle glasses. He wore a brown tweed suit and an old-fashioned cravat-style tie. I could see how Jacob Blaney would have liked him – he was old school.

'I have been a practising psychiatrist at St Brandon's since 1975,' he said, after he was sworn in and stated his name and credentials. 'I began treating Jacob Blaney three weeks later. He came to me as an outpatient, and regularly for weeks and sometimes months at a time as an inpatient from then until he died in 2001.'

'Why did Jacob Blaney require your good offices, doctor?'

'He suffered from paranoid schizophrenia. From what I could piece together he began to exhibit symptoms in his teens. Now, let me be clear: schizophrenia is a difficult disorder to explain – there are many symptoms and every patient is different. Jacob showed all the classic traits: extreme paranoia, auditory and visual hallucinations, violent mood swings and wild erratic behaviours. But he could also have periods of lucidity where he would appear perfectly normal. He was, like all the Blaney men, I suppose, intensely proud of his family heritage and he fought hard to keep his illness a secret.'

'Did you condone this course of action?'

'If people were more open about their mental illness there would be far less stigma attached to it!' Brunswick snapped. 'Of course I didn't. Eventually he agreed to tell his wife. He was adamant that his children were never to find out, and the deal we made was that he would agree to a course of drug treatment – I used neuroleptics – and that he come in to the hospital if his symptoms started to grow severe. I regret that that responsibility fell mostly to his wife, who cared for him selflessly.'

'As Jacob got older, did his condition improve?'

'If anything it got worse. The periods of time he needed to be in full-time care got longer and more regular. His tendency towards violence became much, much greater. I did see some improvement with a new course of drugs, the so-called "atypical antipsychotics" which he did respond well to, but the lessening of symptoms was very slight.'

'Would you say that a man with this level of schizophrenia was of sound mind – *fit to write a will*, for example?'

'That is not a simple question,' Brunswick said. 'I suppose the simplest way to answer it would be to say that, should Jacob Blaney have tried to write his will during a period of illness – when he was in the throes of the disorder – and he was sick far more often than he was well, towards the end; if he were to try and write any kind of legal document under those conditions then no, he would not have been of sound mind.'

'No further questions,' Stephen Horton said.

Keith Dignam stood up. He cut a far less dashing figure than his opposite, but he knew how to hold his own.

'Doctor Brunswick,' Dignam said, pronouncing each syllable slowly. 'You have stated that Mr Blaney, God rest his soul, experienced periods of clear lucidity, when he, and I quote, "could appear quite normal". Doctor, would it be fair to say that, during these periods, Mr Blaney was fully functioning as an individual?'

'If you mean was he capable of carrying out all the normal functions of an adult, then yes, I suppose he was.'

'So during those times he was of sound mind!' Dignam shouted dramatically, spinning to face the doctor.

'No,' Brunswick said, stopping the lawyer in his tracks.

'But you just said—'

'I know what I just said.'

'Will I have it read back to you?'

'That will not be necessary. The simple fact is that, even during those moments of clarity, Jacob's intellectual and logical processing was skewed.'

'Surely that is a matter of conjecture,' Dignam said, trying to make out like it was a joke. 'Come now, doctor, you weren't with him twenty-four hours a day.'

'I wasn't, but I spoke to his wife almost daily while there was still a phone in the house. She told me how things were progressing, and it was very clear that Jacob was descending into a pit of paranoia and depression. I tried to stop it, but he would not listen to me. There were some fixations he had that I could not shift, no matter how hard I tried.'

'What fixations are you referring to here, doctor?'

'In the mid 1980s, Jacob began to think that evil thoughts were being implanted into his head down the telephone. He claimed he could hear another voice when he talked on the phone, telling him to hurt his family. It got so he would not use the phone himself, and his wife had to make all calls for him. Eventually he started to think the bad thoughts were going to get her, too. He was convinced she would be induced by them be poison him. So he got rid of the phone. Gradually, over the course of about six months, the TV went, then the radio, then he had the electricity disconnected and after that the mains water – he wanted nothing travelling into the house from outside, he was convinced any medium could be used to transmit these intrusive thoughts. He effectively walled himself and his family into their little kingdom – cut them off from the outside.'

'Doctor, don't a lot of people choose to live without a

television?' Dignam asked. 'I mean, I barely watch the thing myself. That's not a sign of insanity – many would assert it shows remarkable intelligence.'

'I would applaud anybody who chooses to blow up their television set because it is a source of lethargy and encourages a small-minded view of the world,' Doctor Brunswick said matter-of-factly. 'I would be less enthused by someone who does it because they think the box is telling them – and let me be very clear in this – they believe the television, as an entity, is talking to them directly, not them as part of a large crowd watching the programme they have on, but them, distinctly, one to one. It is talking to them, and telling them to go to their son's room and smother him with a pillow. Despite Tom Blaney's protestations otherwise, he knows that his father tried to do that to him. His mother luckily managed to pull him away before he did permanent damage.'

'That is a lie!' Tom shouted, standing up and lurching towards the stand.

'You are in denial, Mr Blaney,' Doctor Brunswick said. 'You have followed a lifestyle laid out by your father when he was very sick, and you treat it as if it is a sacred trust he passed on to you. Please believe me – his choices were not informed by anything other than a serious mental illness.'

'You don't know what you are talking about!' Tom shouted.

The judge banged his gavel and called for order.

'I think you have gone off topic a little bit,' Keith Dignam said when things had settled down a bit. 'Let me put it to you like this: during one of his periods of lucidity, could Jacob Blaney have participated in the writing of a will that does not, within the legal passages, contain anything outlandish or out of the ordinary. A father leaves the bulk of his estate to his eldest son, but leaves a sizeable amount of money to his younger son. Quite a fair, sane business, I would say.'

'Have you seen the letter he left for Tom?'

'I have, but that was a personal letter, nothing in it was legally binding. Back to the will. I ask you again: during a period of lucidity could Jacob Blaney have – mind fully functional, faculties all intact – could he have overseen the writing of his will?'

Doctor Brunswick paused and took off his glasses, polishing them vigorously with a pocket handkerchief.

'It is possible he may have had a window of lucidity sufficient to do the job, yes.'

'I have no further questions,' Keith Dignam said and sat down.

'Where the hell does that leave us?' I whispered to Chaplin.

'Fucked if I know,' he said.

40

I realized that, with both parents in court, the Blaney children were unsupervised and therefore able to take a visit. I packed my picnic basket with sandwiches and rolls, a cooler full of various juices and soft drinks and a chocolate fudge cake and apple crumble I'd baked the night before. I then drove out to the house.

Jim answered the door. He looked awful – a bruise covered his left cheekbone and he had a tooth missing. It had been three weeks since I had seen him, and he looked rib thin.

'We're not meant to talk to you,' he said, scowling at me. 'Dad says you is a yellow coward traitor and he'd like to string you up by your pinkie.'

'My pinkie?' I said.

'Yeah.'

'Well that doesn't sound very nice,' I agreed. 'Can I come in? I'd like to see the others, and I have some food.'

I saw his eyes drop to the basket I had under my arm.

'Do you?'

'Lots,' I said.

He swung open the door and I left the basket and went to get the cooler and the box with the cakes.

'Let's bring them to the kitchen and we can have a proper meal there,' I said.

I set things up while Jim got his brother and sisters. When I saw them my heart fell. All were hollow-eyed, all showed signs of beatings, and Emma had raw, bald patches in her beautiful hair. I thought I saw the marks of ringworm on Winnie's arm and Dom seemed to have no energy at all – he was sluggish, lethargic – he barely showed any enthusiasm, even for the food.

'Come on, dig in,' I said, passing around plates and offering drinks.

Most of the meal was in silence. The reality was clear: I had lost any bond of trust I had once shared with the children. I had let them down. I couldn't blame them for clamming up on me – and I didn't. These kids had never been given an even break – the world had repeatedly handed them a bum deal, and the abortive Section 12 had been the last straw.

I had heard a story once about an innocent man who had been sentenced to death. Ten years he sat in a cell on Death Row, and finally the day came for his execution. He had no family – or maybe those he did have had given up on him – and he spent his final hours reading and listening to music. He ate a hearty last meal and then made his shuffling, clumsy walk to the death chamber, his ankles in chains. He was strapped down to the table where he would receive the fatal injection, and asked if he had any final words. He simply proclaimed his innocence one last time and said that he had made his peace with God and was ready to die. Then he closed his eyes, and waited for the end.

Just as the button was about to be pushed the telephone rang – there had been a stay of execution, an appeal had been successful. The man was not just not going to die, he was being pardoned: he was to go free.

One would imagine that this would be the most amazing news in the world, but apparently the man was never the same afterwards. He changed from a calm, easy-going, quiet man to an angry, dour, aggressive individual.

Five years later he killed himself.

It seems that he had been ready to die, had prepared himself and, figuratively at least, packed his bags. Coming back from that was more than he could cope with.

I wondered about the Blaney children. Their experience, combined with the effect of the whole thing on their father, had been devastating.

When they had finished eating, the children's mood lifted slightly. I sat Emma on my knee and had a look at her hair. It did not take me long to see that the poor little thing was riddled with head lice – that voracious parasite that makes its living off the blood of its host and can become very debilitating if the infestation gets bad enough.

'You've been scratching a lot, haven't you?' I asked.

'My head been real itchy,' Emma said.

The bald patches had been caused by her ripping at her head to deal with the itch – I had seen it before. Her hair was full of oval white eggs, stuck to the follicles. So far along was the colonization I could see the adults moving about close to her scalp.

'Did you have some visitors out here?' I asked – head lice are passed on by physical contact. The other kids hadn't had them, so where did Emma get them?

'Daddy's lawyer comed out, and his kids was with him,' Emma said. 'They was mean. I din' like them none.'

'Well, unless you caught these off your dad, those kids gave you a nasty present,' I said. 'I better check the rest of you.'

Dom had them too, though nowhere near as bad as Emma, and Winnie did have ringworm, which despite the name is not caused by a worm but is a fungal infection. The child probably had it due to being run-down from stress and lack of food – and the hygiene in the house couldn't have helped.

There was little I could do – all the children needed to be treated with the proper medicinal applications, and Emma and Dom's hair would also need to be treated with a fine comb. I could get these things without any real difficulty, I just wasn't sure how easy it would be to get back out and make sure the children used them.

'I'm sorry about what happened,' I said after I had finished looking the kids over.

'You made Bad Daddy real mad,' Winnie said. 'I don' think I ever seen him so mad as he was that day. He was happy at first when you all went away, but then he got mad again. He shouted so loud, and he hit us. He kept on talking to hisself, sayin' he was the on'y one who understood.'

'He kept talking to himself?'

'Yeah. He'd scream at Jim and box him in the head, and then he'd say, real quiet: "What? No, you know I have to teach him. He's my first born." Stuff like that.'

'What else did he say?'

'He's say: "You told me to look out for enemies. I did all you said, but they still come." '

'And has Bad Daddy been around a lot?'

'Most of the time,' Emma said. 'Good Daddy is hardly ever here now.'

'And you haven't been to school?'

'Not since that day all the men came,' Dom said. 'Iss a pity, 'cause I liked school.'

'I knew it wouldn't last long,' Emma said, scratching thoughtfully.

'You might get to go back yet,' I said.

'Naw,' Jim said. 'We won't. This is how it's gonna be from now on.'

* * *

I parked outside the courthouse and waited. I knew that business for the day would be over at about five, so I only had a few minutes to wait. The public all spilled out first, milling about, sharing their perspectives on what had happened that day. Slowly they dispersed. Gerry Blaney and his team came out, talking rapidly, then Tom, Dignam and their people. I waited. Tom's group wandered off to the side a bit, and then the person I'd been waiting for emerged: Dora. Not waiting for her to take off, I hopped from the car and called over.

'Dora, can I have a word?'

Tom never even looked over at me. I opened the passenger door of the Austin for her and, shrugging, she got in.

'Nice car,' she said. 'I noticed you had a nice ride the last time you were out.'

'Dora,' I said, too annoyed to engage in niceties, 'what the fuck are you thinking?'

'What?' she gasped, blind-sided.

'I went out to see your kids today. Now, do you want me to describe what I saw – cuts, bruises, parasitic infestations, not to mention the fact that they look as if they haven't eaten a bite since the last *fucking time I fed them*!'

'You don't know anything,' Dora hissed.

'What is fucking wrong with you?' I asked. 'Dora, you're not a Blaney, you don't have this bullshit "we came here with the Normans" nonsense they all seem to buy in to. You can be better than that. Look, for right or wrong, you've been given a second chance with your kids. Why in the name of God have you let them get into the state they're in right now?'

'*What about the state I'm in?*' Dora screamed at me all of a sudden. 'None of ye ever cares a damn about me! You have no fucking clue of what I have suffered down through the years.'

244

'Tell me,' I said, catching her hand and squeezing it. 'I'm sitting here right now, asking you to make me understand.'

'You couldn't get your head around it even if I told you,' she spat.

'If you don't talk to me, let me help you find someone else that you can speak to,' I said. 'You aren't in this on your own – your children need you. Do it for them, for fuck's sake.'

'Don't you worry,' she said, opening the door. 'It'll all work out.'

'I'm not so sure about that,' I said.

'I don't fuckin' care what you think,' she said, and was gone.

I didn't wait for Tom to realize what had just happened. I turned on the engine and drove away. As I drove, I had a feeling that I might have caught a glimpse of the truth. The problem was, I had no idea what it was.

'You 'member that story you told me 'bout 'Laddin and that magic lamp?'

The girl and I were lying on our backs watching the clouds, something that had become a favourite pastime of hers.

'I do,' I said. 'It's a good story.'

'I thinked I found a lamp like that in one o' the rubbish rooms in our house.'

'A magic lamp?'

'Yeah. It looks like one, anyway.'

'What you gonna do with it?'

'I hid it. I'm savin' it for jus' the right time.'

'And when will that be?'

'When it all gets so bad, I can' take it no more. Then I'm gonna get the lamp, and rub it, and bring that genie out right fast to give me a wish.'

'That sounds like a good plan,' I said. 'But are you sure there's a genie in that lamp? What if you wait for the right time and then you go running to your lamp and nothing happens? You'll be very upset, won't you?'

'I'm sure. I put my ear to the side of the lamp, and I listened real good, and I could hear him movin' round in there!'

I didn't have an answer to that, so I stayed quiet.

'Want to know what I'm gonna wish?' she asked after a bit.

'Tell me,' I said.

'I'm gonna ask for me and my brothers and sister to be whisked off to a beautiful island, with a beach, and a nice house to live in and all the food we can eat and lots of games.'

'That sounds really nice,' I said.

'An' you can come and visit me,' she said.

'Can I?'

'Yeah. Each of us can have one friend. You can be mine.'

'Sweetie, I'm very flattered,' I said, and I really was.

'One o' these days, I'm gonna do it,' she said. 'One o' these days.'

41

Rachel's phone made a beeping sound, and the screen flashed.

A message had been delivered, and the number it came from flashed up on the screen too – it was Jeff McKinney's number.

Rachel, as it happened, didn't have her phone. She had, at my request, loaned it to me for a few days. When this message came in, I was sitting in the staff room at the school – class was to start in a couple of hours. I opened the message, read the first line and stopped. The author had cut to the chase fairly quickly, and I didn't need to ingest any more of his lurid prose. Suffice it to say his intentions were unpleasant and maybe not even legal.

I stood and walked to the door and down the stairs, stopping halfway down, on the first landing. There was Jeff, parked in the lobby, busily fiddling with his own phone. I kept my eye on him, and rang the number that had just sent the disturbing message.

Nothing at first, then I heard a ring at my end. McKinney's phone didn't ring – then it did. He jumped, clearly surprised. He looked at the handset for several long moments, then slowly brought the phone to his ear.

'Hello,' he said shakily.

'Hello Jeff,' I said. 'Guess who?'

Pause. I could see his mind working furiously. He seemed unable to work out what had happened.

'Who is this?' he said at last.

'It's the guy who teaches the class full of little whores,' I said, walking down the stairs towards him. 'As you know, you just sent one of your delightful, colourful little vignettes to this phone, which belongs to a friend of mine who would like you to stop.'

I reached the bottom step.

'This girl,' I hung up and held the phone up to him. 'This girl *is* prepared to go to the cops and to show your handiwork to George Taylor. But she still feels a little sorry for you. The soft thing, she wants to give you a chance: stop sending her, and everyone else, your filthy messages or she *will* go to the authorities.'

Jeff, his lower lip trembling furiously, never gave me a chance to negotiate. He let out a wail of fright and dismay and bolted out the front door.

'I'm going to take that as a sign of agreement,' I said to the empty hallway, and went to my classroom.

Gladys and I had been meeting for an hour (or as close to it as she managed to get) every Wednesday since that first night. My assessment of her had proved more or less correct. She was, according to an educational psychologist she had gone to for a few sessions, dyslexic with dyspraxic tendencies (although what this last term meant I was not sure).

Gladys's dyslexia showed up most in her handwriting, but I had shown her how to use the word-processing programs on the computers in the school, and with a little practice on the spell-checker we had managed to eradicate a lot of the telltale signs.

Her fear of reading was another issue, however, and that was the main reason we met. I had already learned that she had no fear at all of celebrity gossip magazines and tabloid newspapers, but broadsheets, books of any kind and anything, even a magazine, with the slightest hint of intellectualism sent her into a complete spin, during which she was utterly incapable of reading anything.

We always started out easy, with something she was familiar and comfortable with – this might be a children's story, an article from *OK* or the horoscope from the *Sun*. This particular evening, I had brought the *Western News* along with me. I reasoned she had seen it in her house every week growing up and would feel secure enough with it.

'Pick whatever story interests you the most from this and read it to me,' I said, laying the paper open on the desk between us.

'Whatever I want?'

'You choose.'

'Everyone's talkin' about the Blaney thing. Can I read about that?'

'If you like. There's about twenty pages on it in this week's edition, so you won't be stuck for choice.'

'Of course, I am sort of related to the Blaneys,' Gladys said, winking at me.

'Is that so?' I said, sounding credulous – saying you were related to the Blaneys in Garshaigh was like claiming to be related to the royal family in England.

'Oh yeah. Well, when I say I'm related to the Blaneys, it's the wife I'm related to.'

'Dora?'

'Yeah. She's me cousin. Dora Pointer is her maiden name.'

This knocked me for six.

'You serious? She's your first cousin?'

'Yeah. Used to know her really well. We all kind of lost touch with her in the last five or six years. I think stuff got a bit weird for her, y'know?'

'How do you mean?'

'Well,' Gladys settled down to tell her story, leaning back in her chair and swinging her legs. 'Dora was always the smart one in her family. She done real well at school, straight As right the way across the board – even in Irish! She wasn't the best lookin', but she was *nice* if you know what I mean. She could talk, knew how to present herself. Her ma and da – my da's brother is her da, obviously – her ma and da weren't rich or anything, but they worked hard and they saved their money and they sent her off to college. She trained to be a teacher – did ya know that?'

'I did,' I said. 'How'd she meet Tom Blaney?'

'Now, now, good things come to those who wait,' she laughed, waggling her finger at me. 'She went to St Patrick's teacher training college in Dublin. As far as I know she lived on campus, never went out on the tear or nothin' like that. Got the best degree you can get – straight As again. She got a job in the primary school in Toberclancy, ten miles over. I heard she was doin' great, the kids all loved her. And then the school had a fundraisin' evenin' – a dinner dance I think it was – and Tom Blaney was invited.'

'Love at first sight?'

'I think it was for her. Tom isn't George Clooney, but he has . . . um . . . what do you call it . . .'

'Charisma?'

'That's the one. They started goin' out. From what I heard they never spent any time in his place, always met out or at her home. So she got these ideas about what the Blaney mansion was like. I remember her calling to see me ma one time, and she was all full of what her life was going to be like when they got married – how Tom was goin' to look after her. She'd have the best of everything.'

'Were you at the wedding?'

'No.'

'Your mum and dad?'

'No. Do you know what? *Her* ma 'n' da weren't even at it. I don't even know there ever was a weddin'. We were all *told* they got married, but let me tell you, Dora kept awful fuckin' quiet about the whole thing after that. She gave up her job, moved out to that house and that was that.'

'But you stayed close to her?'

'She would call in from time to time. But almost as soon as she got married, she changed. It was like a piece of her got left behind or broken. Like, Dora was always a little bit full of herself, always wanted to tell you about her latest 'complishments. She wasn't pretty but she always had nice clothes that fit her well and the right colour in her hair for the time of year.'

'There's a right colour for different times of year?'

'Oh yeah. After she got married, she stopped bothering. I remember her ma, me auntie, saying that, sure, she didn't *need* to bother anymore, 'cause she had her man. But that didn't wash with me.'

'Why not?'

'Dora would want to rub all our noses in it. That was the way she was. If she married some rich bastard, she'd want to be visiting us dressed in an outfit none of us could afford, reeking of the most expensive perfume imaginable, with the best haircut and finely manicured nails, telling us about the super amazing holiday she'd be going on next month.'

'And that didn't happen?'

'Shane, when she called, at first, she was just scruffy – none of her clothes were new, and they all looked creased and crumpled. Her hair looked as if it could do with some product in it, and she seemed tired. The next time I saw her she was beyond scruffy. She was *dirty*. She smelt and her face was a mess of spots.'

'That's not good,' I said.

'She would never talk about him, about Tom. She got pregnant, but there was no joy in it. The last time she visited, I came in and she had been talkin' to my ma, and I saw she had been cryin'. I offered to go out, but she said no, she was leavin'. I remember she said to me ma: "I'll make sure Gerry gets that document." And me ma said: "You have to look after yourself, Dora. Those children are all Blaneys, and he'll never let them go. But it's not too late to save yourself." They hugged and Dora left, and I never saw her again.'

'She said she was going to give a document to Gerry,' I said. 'And this was – what – five years ago.'

'Yeah. Maybe a bit less.'

My head was spinning. But I couldn't do anything about it just then.

'Okay, chatterbox,' I laughed. 'Have you picked something to read yet?'

'What about one you wrote?'

'If you don't pick one soon you'll be reading to the whole class!'

So she read me one of my own articles on the court proceedings, and I pondered the slowly forming picture of what was really going on in the tormented world of the Blaneys.

42

I sat with Sid Doran and Josephine Welch in a meeting room in the offices of child services.

'Jacob Blaney, Tom's father, was schizophrenic,' I said. 'It doesn't matter what Tom says, the facts are irrefutable. There are years of records supporting what Gerry is saying.'

'So?' Josephine said. 'That means nothing to us.'

'Schizophrenia has a hereditary element,' I said. 'Listen to what the children have been saying: *Good Daddy* and *Bad Daddy* – the man goes through phases when his personality changes utterly, when he is just not the same man. They told me recently that he talks to his father – and not like a prayer the way any of us might talk to a deceased loved one in a moment of crisis, but as if his father is talking back. He's hearing voices. He is clearly paranoid, convinced people are out to get him, out to do him harm. I believe that Doctor Brunswick was saying as much to Tom in court that first day. He is ill too. And the children are suffering, and have been for years.'

'What you're saying may be true,' Sid said, taking copious notes as he was wont to do. 'But where do we go with it? How do we use this to help us?'

254

'Gerry and Dora are using it,' I said. 'They're trying to drive him to breaking point.'

'Gerry and Dora?' Josephine said, looking at *me* as if I was mad. 'His brother and his wife?'

'Dora gave Gerry the information about Jacob being ill. When the old man died, all his papers were given to Tom. Tom put them away and didn't pay them much heed. Remember, he and Gerry had little idea of how sick their father was, because he wanted it hidden from them. But Dora, she's a teacher, she's bookish, so she tries to put some shape on the records. She told me herself that she had tried to use them to put together a book for the kids about their family heritage, maybe even please Tom. I think she found the details of Jacob's illness then. When living with Tom the way he insisted upon got too much for her, she went to Gerry and gave him the ammunition he needed to make Tom sell the house and the land – thereby freeing her.'

'You have proof of this?'

'I have it from a reliable source,' I said.

'But it's gotten so nasty,' Sid said. 'The thugs, the threats . . .'

'The threats were meant to increase Tom's paranoia, I think. If you remember, Dora was never really threatened, and the only child who was actually outwardly involved was Jim, as the oldest boy. I believe they wanted Tom to get more and more wound up and hopefully have a complete breakdown. But then things went wrong.'

'You made the referral.'

'Yep. Having the kids put in care was never a part of what Dora wanted. I think she hoped to take them with her when she finally had Tom committed. So when it looked as if they were going to be taken by you guys, she got Gerry to use all his influence to put a stop to it.'

'And he did, too,' Sid said, underlining something sharply.

'But he realized it might not hold. So he had me almost beaten up and had the bishop warn me off on pains of losing my job. But you see there is one factor neither she nor Gerry could control.'

'Which is?' Josephine asked.

'Tom's schizophrenia,' I said. 'He's much closer to breaking than any of them had expected, and he is, literally, killing the children, maybe Dora too. They've done it, they've destroyed him. But I am telling you this: those kids need to come out *now*. I'm not saying Dora shouldn't come with them. Frankly, I don't care as long as you get them out.'

'I think we have enough to get the injunction overturned,' Josephine said.

'I think we have more than enough,' Sid said.

'Call me,' I said.

'Don't worry, we'll keep you posted.'

43

The injunction was overturned later that day.

About ten minutes after that case was lost, Gerry won in his civil dispute against his brother. You win some and you lose some, I suppose.

Tom went berserk in the courtroom. He overturned the table in front of him, threw a chair at the judge and jabbered loudly to his long-dead father. Luckily Doctor Brunswick was there and calmly sedated him. Robert Chaplin was so excited by this ending to what had been the most dramatic three days of his life that he spent the night in the office writing.

I was less excited, but it had not escaped me that this would make the children's move easier. As the crowd milled about the courtroom I got a message on my phone. Paying no heed to the number, I opened the message and began to read. My eyes grew wide. I blushed. Closing the message, I checked the number. I didn't recognize it, but I thought I recognized the style of the author. Jeff McKinney, it seemed, was an equal opportunities pervert. Gender was not a barrier where his attentions were concerned.

Dora sat opposite Josephine, Sid and myself in a vacant office in the hospital.

'Your husband had been committed, Mrs Blaney,' Josephine said matter-of-factly. 'He seems to have had a very severe breakdown – his grasp on reality has fractured, somewhat.'

'It's been fractured for a long time,' Dora said without much feeling. 'For as long as I've known him, anyhow.'

'That's for you to come to terms with,' Sid said. 'The most important factor in all this is your children. We are faced with a significant question: should they continue living in your care?'

'Why is that even in question?' Dora asked.

'Because they are likely to be spending the next fortnight in this hospital recovering from the treatment they have had to endure over the past months.'

'All at the hands of my mentally deranged husband,' Dora said sulkily.

'I am prepared to accept that the beatings and *some* of the sexual abuse was down to him, Mrs Blaney,' Sid said, 'but the starvation, the atrocious hygiene, the failure to deal with basic things like nits – I know you were the primary caregiver. That is neglect at its worst. And that falls at your feet.'

'He wouldn't let me feed them,' Dora said, still with no feeling or even a hint of remorse. 'He checked the food before he left and again when he came back. If anything was gone, we all got it.'

'I see no bruises on *you*,' Josephine said. 'Yet your children are black and blue, all of them.'

'He raped me, but wouldn't hit me,' Dora deadpanned. 'He didn't want me marked – not physically, anyway. Sometimes he made me sleep with Jim. But I never touched him, I swear. I'm not like that. Even though he tried to make me that way.'

Josephine sighed and riffled through her papers.

'When the hospital signs them out, the children will be returned to your care, Mrs Blaney. I am assigning a family support worker to you, however. Do you know what that means?'

'No, and I don't think I want to.'

'It means that a worker will be sent out to your home for something in the region of eighteen hours a week to help you with things like behaviour management of the children, finance, diet and food, hygiene, getting the electricity turned back on – that type of thing.'

'And I have no choice in this?'

'No Mrs Blaney, you do not,' Josephine said. 'If you refuse the worker entry, we will simply go to court and get a supervision order. You can get your brother-in-law to try and get that process derailed, but I expect he would find such a petition less well received this time around.'

'That will be all, Mrs Blaney,' Sid said. 'Do you need me to call you a taxi back out home, or are you able to drive?'

'I don't want to go back out to that house,' Dora said, and for the first time there was real fear and pain in her voice.

'You are quite safe,' Josephine said. 'Your husband will not be getting out without your knowing about it.'

'That's not it,' Dora said. 'I don't want to be in that dark, damp hole on my own.'

'Why not?' Josephine asked.

'Because the place freaks me out, that's why!' Dora snapped back, clearly genuinely upset.

Josephine looked at Sid, eyebrows raised.

'I'll see if I can book you in to a room in The Grapevine for a few nights,' Sid said. 'And we should also see if we can get you access to the family bank accounts. Things like hotel rooms need to be paid for. Let's go, then, shall we?'

Sid and Dora left. Josephine picked up her sheaf of paper and straightened it.

'Happy?' she asked me.

'As I can be, under the circumstances,' I said.

'You were uncharacteristically quiet,' she said.

'I had no right to say anything,' I said. 'I have no authority. Besides, Sid tends to say what I would, most of the time.'

'Very *simpatico*,' Josephine said.

'Yeah. I'm going to see the kids,' I said.

'Off you go then.'

I left her to her paper straightening and her sarcasm. It was starting to wear me out.

44

Emma was lying in a foetal position in bed when I found her. She was in a ward full of children, but the curtain had been left pulled around her, and she seemed isolated and very small and vulnerable.

'Hey Emma,' I said, pulling a chair over to her bedside. 'How are you?'

Her eyes were open and she looked right at me, but there was only heartache in her eyes. I saw that her hair had been cut quite short and anti-louse lotion had been put through it. It managed to smell sweet and bitter all at the same time.

'I like what they've done to your hair,' I lied. 'Are you pleased with it?'

She shook her head, and I saw her eyes fill with tears.

'Hey,' I said gently. 'Would you like a cuddle?'

She nodded and I reached out to her and she came to me and sobbed bitterly as I rocked her like a baby.

A long time later she asked:

'What goin' t' happen t'us?'

'You're all going to stay in hospital for a little bit, until you get well again, and then you're going to live with your mum.'

'Wha' 'bout Daddy?'

'Your dad is sick in his mind,' I said. 'He has to stay in a special hospital for a while. Maybe a long while.'

'Where Dom?'

'In a room about two minutes away from here. Want to go see him?'

'No. Soon, maybe.'

She snuggled back down into me. I kept my arms wrapped about her.

'Can I have somet'in' t' eat?'

'Sure can,' I said. 'I'll ring the nurse.'

I did, and some toast and juice were secured for the little girl. When the food came (and the considerate nurse brought some coffee for me), Emma said, around bites of toast and jam:

'Mammy gonna feed us now?'

'Yes,' I said. 'There will be somebody coming to spend time with you all to make sure she does.'

'Who?'

'I don't know yet,' I said. 'But I know you'll like them. They'll help you all to make a better life for yourselves.'

'You come see us too?'

'Try and keep me away!' I laughed. 'Of course I'll come and see you.'

'We play games an' all? Like before?'

'Lots of games. And you'll have TV and the radio and maybe a video game or two, as well.'

She paused, her mouth full.

'What TV like?'

'Well, it's like a magic box that shows you pictures and tells you stories, and there's music and colours, and you're going to probably watch far too much of it!'

She giggled and drank some juice.

262

'Shane?'

'Yes, sweetie.'

'I don' tink Mammy ever really liked us all that much.'

'Oh,' I said, not entirely surprised at this statement.

'Yeah. She di'n't give us much food, even when Bad Daddy not around. An' when we cried, she never hugged us or nothin'. Never talked to us much.'

'Well,' I said. 'If your mum was scared all the time, and that could make her maybe forget how to show you she loved you. Being really unhappy can do that, you know.'

'Can it?'

'Yeah. And I think your mum was very unhappy for a very long time.'

'How we make her happy again?'

'Well, that's something to work on with your new worker. But it can be done. You just need to teach her how to be a good mum.'

Emma had finished her toast and was sucking hard on the straw that protruded from her juice carton. When she was sure it was empty, she placed it carefully down on her plate.

'We go see Dom now?'

I held out my hand and she took it.

'I wants to tell him all about the TV,' she said gleefully.

They had a wonderful conversation about it. I wondered for a time if it was healthy to have them placing so much hope on something so crass and mindless. I could hear Jacob Blaney rumbling away in rage somewhere in my subconscious. But I eventually decided I didn't care, and just enjoyed the simple joy of two kids who had just emerged from a terrible darkness.

45

I kept getting the text messages.

I checked with Jessie and Rachel and Carla, and their inboxes had been uncontaminated by McKinney's attentions for many months. It seemed that my interference had stopped him from bothering my students, but had for some reason attracted him to me.

I called in to The Grapevine. The manageress peered at me over the counter.

'You back?' she asked. 'It's the same price for the dog.'

'No, thank you. I want to see Jeff McKinney.'

'Wheelie? He's gone, thank God. Bloody nuisance, always hangin' around, gettin' under me feet.'

'What, did you sack him?'

'You can't sack someone you don't employ.'

I didn't know what to say.

'So he never worked here?'

'I let him sleep in a little cubbyhole out the back. His parents fucked off and left him when he was thirteen or so without a bite of bread in the cupboard or a penny to his name. The house was fallin' apart, not fit for a dog to live in. He came here lookin' for work, but sure, I didn't have anything for him to do – I felt sorry for him and gave him somewhere to stay, let him take his meals with the staff.'

'That was very generous of you,' I said.

'I always thought he'd grow up and move on. He never did, though. He just got older and stranger.'

'Stranger?'

'He was always watchin'. You'd go into a room and you'd be doin' some work there, and the next thing you'd realize he'd been there the whole time, sittin', watchin' you. I've gotten I don't know how many complaints from staff and guests.'

'Why didn't you just throw him out?' I asked.

'You know why,' she said. 'He's in a wheelchair. He's got special needs.'

'That doesn't mean he can't be an asshole,' I said.

I changed my number.

The messages stopped.

Gladys Pointer passed all her exams.

Technically I should have just handed all the details over to the school's administrative office so they could send out her results along with everybody else's, but I couldn't wait to let her know. So I got her phone number from her file and asked her to meet me in the café for lunch.

'What's up?' she asked as she sat down.

'What do you want to eat?' I asked her. 'This is my treat.'

'Oh – um, well, the toasted special. And a cappuccino.'

I handed her the envelope with her results in it.

'You have a look at that while I order.'

I went up to the counter and gave the girl (it was Carla's day off) our order, then went back to Gladys, who was pouring over the page.

'What does it mean?' she asked, not looking too happy.

'It means you not only passed everything,' I said, 'but that you got honours in everything, too. And not only did you get honours in everything, you got a Distinction, which is like an A, in two of the four subjects you studied. You did fantastically well, Gladys. You should be really proud of yourself.'

'But . . . how?' Gladys asked, almost speechless.

'You worked incredibly hard,' I said. 'You faced up to the difficulties you had and you overcame them. You also found something you like and you really care about and you gave it a hundred per cent, a hundred per cent of the time. That makes a big difference, I think.'

'Did you go easy on me?' she asked, looking genuinely terrified to ask. 'You know, because we get on and all that.'

'Are you asking me if I gave you an easy ride?' I asked.

'Yeah. I have to know, Shane. This year has half killed me. My ma keeps tellin' me she'll be proud no matter how I do – *like she's expectin' me to fail!* Tell me the truth, Shane. Please.'

'I treated your work the exact same as I did everyone else's,' I said in as calm and gentle a voice as I could muster. 'I did not go any *harder* on you, but I didn't go any *easier* either. No, you deserve the grades you got.'

'D'ya *swear?*'

'Honest injun,' I said, and without warning she flung herself across the table and hugged me fiercely. 'Thank you,' she said, half crying and half laughing. 'Thank you so much.'

'You did the work, Gladys, not me!' I said, patting her on the back and laughing too. 'All I did was point you in the right direction.'

'I couldn't have done it without you,' she said, sitting back down and rubbing her eyes.

'I think you were ready to do the work,' I said. 'I just happened to be in the right place at the right time.'

'Thank you,' she said again.

'It was my privilege,' I said truthfully.

46

The Blaney homestead and all the land attached to it was sold to the Midden Development Group lock, stock and barrel one month after the court case. Jacob Blaney's will had been deemed null and void, and that meant his estate was to be liquidated and the profits divided. Gerry very decently gave Dora and the children three-quarters of the money earned, and they bought a modest house in Garshaigh.

The good people at Midden published their plans for the land in the *Western News*. The entire fifty acres were to be turned into a massive shopping centre with a cinema, a bowling alley, a paintball arena and every kind of shop and restaurant imaginable. It would bring a lot of business and employment to the region.

I expected either widespread condemnation for the scheme or else unanimous support. Instead we got neither. I sat in the office the day after the plans were made public, expecting a shitstorm of indignation, but none arrived. It was as if people just weren't that bothered by the news, as if it mattered little to them. I was amazed. Maybe there was something in it all that I was missing – as people kept reminding me: I was a blow-in.

*   *   *

One week later I was at my desk alone – Chaplin was covering the courts that day, and I was writing the obituaries, a grim but necessary job for any local paper. Suddenly the door opened and Gerry Blaney came in, carrying two Styrofoam cups of coffee.

'They tell me down below you drink it black,' he said.

'They tell you right,' I said. 'To what do I owe this dubious pleasure?'

He handed me my cup and sat down opposite me, making a big deal out of taking the lid off his, applying sugar and milk from those little plastic cartons that hold about two spoonfuls. I watched him, feeling nothing but distaste for the little man – he had done little but make my life difficult since I first encountered him.

'How are those kiddies doing?' he asked when he was content with his coffee.

'Quite well, all things considered,' I said. 'They're out of hospital now, and I'm told they're building a relationship with their mother slowly but surely. They are a really wonderful bunch of children.'

'Dora's not such a bad skin either, if you give her a chance,' Gerry said.

I looked at him.

'What is the deal between you and her?'

'The deal? Whatever do you mean?'

'You know what I mean, Gerry.'

'Would you believe me if I said I felt sorry for her?'

I almost choked on my coffee.

'I would find that very hard to believe,' I said.

'Why so?'

'It does not fit what I know of your character.'

Gerry grinned. It was not a pleasant thing to see.

'And is it possible, even remotely, that you have misjudged me?'

'Anything is possible,' I admitted.

'She was a young girl from a well-off, sheltered background who fell hook, line and sinker for the *legend* of the Blaneys. Let me tell you, Shane, that is a myth that has been dead and decomposing for a long time. I don't know if she ever really paid any attention to Tom when they were courtin'. By the time he brought her out to the house and more or less imprisoned her there, it was too late.'

'So you and her hatched this plan to sell the place out from under him?'

'It was her idea. She's a resourceful girl. I agreed to help.'

'For no personal gain, obviously.'

He made a 'little bit of this, little bit of that' wobble with his hand.

'I never said that.'

'Well, it worked out well from my end, anyway,' I said, 'if you ignore the threatened beatings, the near sackings from my teaching post and the added trauma for the children. Goddam it Gerry, what the fuck was going through your mind?'

'I regret some of those things,' he said.

'Some of them?'

He took a piece of paper from his inside pocket and handed t to me.

'That's a copy, you can keep it,' he said.

'What is it?'

'You're an investigative journalist,' he said. 'Why don't you ry reading it?'

I unfolded the page. It was a protection order for the house nd land Gerry had just sold to Midden Development. It neant that nothing could be done to a single blade of grass on

269

those fifty acres. Not so much as a shovel could be put into the ground. I noted that the order was dated 1998.

'Did you know about this?' I asked.

'Of course.'

'But you didn't think to tell the company you just sold the land to for millions and millions of euro.'

'They can try and get it overturned.'

'But they won't be successful.'

'No. Not on that land. Far too much history on a tract of countryside that really hasn't been changed – well, *ever*.'

I looked at the order and shook my head.

'You are some piece of work, Gerry Blaney,' I said.

'Thank you,' he said, standing up. 'You're not exactly a shrinking violet yourself. You wouldn't back down, would you?'

'I did consider it,' I said. 'Let's just say a little voice in my head wouldn't let me.'

'You look out for yourself,' he said. 'And I'd appreciate it if you kept an eye on my nieces and nephews.'

'Or you could look in on them yourself once in a while,' I suggested.

He smiled, a more pleasant expression this time.

'Maybe,' he said, and left me.

I sat and reread the preservation order. I realized that even though the land had, for the first time in a millennium, changed hands, it was still to all intents and purposes Blaney land. I also suspected that Gerry had plans to buy it back for a fraction of the price for which it had been sold.

And the cycle would continue.

47

I locked the door of my class and switched off the light in the hallway.

'You finished then, Shane?' George Taylor asked as I passed through the lobby.

'Don't you ever go home, Mr Taylor?' I asked.

'This is my home, in a way,' he said.

'Well, you have a good night,' I said. 'I'll probably see you over the summer – I daresay I'll be in and out, preparing for next year's classes.'

'I would expect no less,' he said, leafing through some sheets on the clipboard he was carrying. 'I may have some hours during the day next year – would you be at all interested?'

'I might,' I said. 'How many are we talking about?'

'Maybe twelve – maybe more. I'm not a hundred per cent certain as yet.'

'I'm still not going to cut my hair,' I said.

'I know that,' he said, and I thought I saw just the touch of a smile.

'Let's talk when you have all the information,' I said.

'Let's do that. See you soon.'

And I left him to his ruminations.

* * *

The beach that summer night was calm and cool. Millie ran her concentric circles for a while, sniffed about for a time, then lay down beside me, panting heavily. I watched the waves coming in: steady, interminable, relentless. Behind me across the fields and trees, occupied now by badgers and foxes and a colony of long-eared bats, sat the ancient Blaney house with its dust and its madness and its shadows. I wondered if anyone would ever live there again, or if Gerry would eventually have it demolished. Maybe he would allow the land to go to seed, and the very countryside itself would reclaim the house.

I felt someone sit down on the other side of Millie, looked over, and there was Lonnie Whitmore.

'Where have you been?' I asked. 'There's been a lot of stuff going down, you know. Might have been nice to have you around for a little backup.'

'You don't need me around anymore, and you know it,' Lonnie said, his hand resting on Millie's flank. 'I'm not sure you ever did to begin with.'

'You know I did,' I said, looking at him. 'You were my best friend. That's no small thing for me to say, Lonnie.'

'I'll always be your friend,' he said. 'Death doesn't change that.'

'No?'

'No. We are the things we have done. We are the difference we made. We are the impact we had on the lives of people around us. You changed me, Shane. Made me better. That doesn't stop.'

'I think we made one another better,' I said.

He sat, mostly in shadow – I could just see his thick, untidy hair and his heavy brow.

'You going to stay in Garshaigh?' he asked.

'I think so. I'll give it another year, anyway. I can't leave the

Blaney kids, and I like the newspaper and the classes. I think some of the locals are even starting to accept me.'

'People want to accept you, you know,' he said. 'You need to learn to let them. Start seeing the world with optimism. Hope. There's enough darkness in it. Let yours go.'

'I will,' I said. Then: 'I miss you.'

'I know. Thank you for missing me. But I have to go.'

'I know that.'

He stood up. Millie stirred, standing up, shaking herself. He stroked her head.

'Goodbye, dog,' he said, and began to walk towards the ocean.

Millie whined and went to follow him.

'Stay,' he said, holding his hand out in warning.

Whimpering, she complied.

Lonnie turned back to me one last time.

'Be happy,' he said and, saluting us both, walked down the beach to the eddying sea, leaving no tracks as he passed. Before he reached the water he was gone.

I held Millie and sobbed inconsolably. The greyhound lay against me, and as my crying eased she licked my tears away.

'He loved you, you know,' I said. 'And I know you loved him.'

She watched me as if she understood every word I said.

He loved us both.

I got home around midnight. I reached for the whiskey bottle but then changed my mind. I made some tea and, with my dog snuggled against me, watched Tom Selleck as *Magnum PI*, racing around Hawaii in a bright red Ferrari.

It was a funny episode. I laughed. I think Millie did too.

I slept the night through, and awoke to find the following day beautiful and sunny.

'Hi,' the girl said.

'Hey.'

'I rubbed the lamp.'

'Did you? Did the genie come out?'

'Not right away, but I made the wish anyway.'

'Did it work?'

She sat on the couch in her new home, wearing a bright blue dress. Her hair, much shorter now, was clean and smelt of peaches. The bald patches were scarcely noticeable, and it was the first time I had ever seen her wearing shoes.

'I didn't think it did, at first,' she said.

'At first?'

'Yeah. The men came and took me. I ran to the hideout we made, but they found me there and took me. And then I was in the hospital, and that was rotten. But then they brought us to this house, and it's clean and beautiful, and Shona comes to see us every day to make sure Mam feeds us. And look!'

She picked up a remote control and hit a button and a television in the corner blazed into life. To my delight the girl burst into excited laughter.

'We have a telly!' she squealed, unable to contain her joy. 'Just like you said we would!'

'So maybe you were right about the genie,' I said. 'Looks like you got everything you wished for, doesn't it?'

'You know what the biggest part of my wish was?'

'What?'

'That I wouldn't be afraid no more.'

'How's that bit going?'

'Goin' pretty good.'

'I'm glad, Emma.'

We sat in the strange, shiny new living room for a while, grinning at one another.

'So what do you want to do then,' I asked. 'We can watch some TV, listen to some music, play your brand spanking new Xbox . . .'

Emma laughed nervously.

'Know what I'd like to do?'

'What?'

'I'd like to play Cloud Shapes.'

For some reason, I felt tears come to my eyes at that.

'I'd like that too,' I said.

We went out into the sunshine.

As we lay watching the sky I remembered her earlier comment: 'You said the genie didn't come right away?'

'No. I din' see him until they was carryin' me off.'

'But you saw him then?'

'One of de men had me over his shoulder so I was lookin' back, away from him. I seen a little man, dressed all in mad colours. He had sticky-up hair and a thick forehead. He was standin' in the door to our hideout and he was smilin' at me and he said to me that I had my wish, and not to be afraid. It would be all right. And you know what?'

'What?' I said, feeling the words catch in my throat.

'I knew he was tellin' me the truth.'

She fumbled about and found my hand and held it.

And we lay and watched clouds until the sun set.

AFTERWORD

The Girl from Yesterday is a book that in many ways wrote itself. It revealed its mysteries to me a piece at a time as I wrote it at breakneck speed the week I celebrated my fortieth birthday. This might sound strange for a book that sits in the non-fiction section of your bookstore or library, but in actuality the layers of this complex story were not clear to me when I started writing – I *thought* I knew what had happened, but discovered as I returned to Garshaigh and its wild, ancient countryside that I didn't know the half of it. Writing can be a cathartic experience, but it can also be a revelatory one. The truth is (and I have really tried to portray plainly that I was a bystander in many elements of the Blaney case – an observer, really) that the motivations of many of the players are still a mystery to me, even now. I hope you get something from trying to pick apart the mixed, muddled and in some parts ridiculous aspects of it all. It was certainly fun sifting through the murk again, with the benefit of hindsight.

It was fun, but it was painful, too.

I had never been involved in a child protection case as an observer before, as someone with no authority and no real capacity to affect what happened. I was lucky to end up working with Sid Doran, who was, I believe, much more courteous to me than I would have been to him in similar circumstances. I am, occasionally, accused of arrogance and having a hero complex in book reviews and general conversation, but a surefire way of knocking those two flaws out of your personality is to find yourself in the child protection system as a member of the public. It can be a real leveller. My experience with Sid taught me that there are many people who deserve care in any interaction between a family and the system, not just the children and the workers themselves. For that lesson, I am eternally grateful.

Emma, Dom, Winnie and Jim are doing well now. They courageously set about the difficult task of learning to be a family, along with their mother Dora, despite the horrors of their lives up to that point. I can attest to the fact that they had a wonderful family support worker in Shona Grant, and she helped them through a lot of tears, much doubt and several occasions when it looked as if the whole thing would come crashing down about them. All the children struggled at school, but again, with the patience of some talented teachers and a willingness to go that extra mile, they are making headway.

I will freely admit that I harboured a lot of resentment to Nathalie Lassiter for her shock turnabout, and I can also attest that, when I have run into her in the years since, I have nodded a hello and kept going. Yet I do understand why she decided to throw her lot in with Gerry Blaney, and why she signed that petition that had such a devastating impact on our attempt to remove the children from harm. I even think that, somewhere in her head, she thought she was doing the right thing. God knows, I was going through a lot of doubt myself at that stage of my life, wondering if I had any right to do some of the things I had done in the name of child protection in the past. Family is such a sacred thing, and anything that interferes with that has to be looked at gravely. I think that Nathalie was certainly put under pressure by Gerry and his cronies, but I also think she examined her own conscience and came to believe that perhaps such an invasive approach might not be the right path to take.

I cannot blame her for that.

Emma, who is at the centre of this story, and through whose eyes we see much of what is going on, is one of those children who touched my heart deeply. There is about her something so incredibly gentle, yet profoundly strong, so wilful yet unbelievably sensitive. She is a child with an old soul, I think. She will be an adult to be reckoned with.

Tom Blaney never came out of the psychiatric hospital. Dora visits him. His children choose not to do so.

Gladys Pointer is one of the best students I have ever taught. Despite her difficulties she went on to graduate with Distinction from her FETAC Level 5, and went on to further studies. She now runs a large community childcare centre near Garshaigh and is a gifted childcare worker. She and I keep in touch, and it is always a pleasure to hear her irreverent take on life and her stories about the ups and downs of working in the huge crèche she runs – I often envy her the work she does; it sounds like such fun!

The truth of Gladys's story is that education, which is, I believe, the birthright of every single person, can be a deeply distressing experience if you are not lucky enough to be 'average'. Gladys's difficulties were not even that extreme or unusual – a little help would have been enough to get her through her school exams with flying colours. Yet somewhere along the line a callous teacher said some cruel things, and a young girl who was actually very bright was left believing that she was stupid and worthless. It angers me that, in this day and age, children are still being subjected to this sort of

Dickensian treatment. This is, I feel, utterly criminal. I am delighted that Gladys was able to rise above such small-mindedness and reach her true potential.

George Taylor is one of those men who somehow fits the stereotype (look up the words *principal* or *headmaster* in the dictionary, and you may well find a picture of George), yet he also surpasses it in almost every way. He is a man of supreme intelligence, incredible loyalty and a great sense of humour. I remain grateful for the chances he gave me. I know beyond any doubt that had those thugs decided, as Mr Taylor put it, to *throw down fisticuffs*, he would have responded in kind. In his world, if a member of his staff is threatened, his job is to stand side by side with them, come what may. If I ever find myself in a pub brawl, George Taylor is certainly someone I would like to have on my side.

I toyed with the idea of not telling the story of Jeff McKinney in this book, even though it was certainly a part of what happened. I felt certain that many readers would feel I was picking on someone with a disability. And *that* is the reason I finally decided to put it in here: you see, the fact that Jeff McKinney was in a wheelchair is inconsequential. The truth is that he was a predator – he worked his way into the lives of vulnerable young women and he then abused their trust. His disability is simply a facet of his physical description – it did not *cause* him to do the things he did.

George Taylor, for all his integrity, could not find it in his heart to fire Jeff, although he did confront him. Jessie and Carla could not go to the police because they felt sorry for him. The manageress of the hotel who had taken him in could not evict him, despite his antisocial behaviour. All felt trapped by the fact that, as a person with a disability, he deserved our charity and our pity. In truth, well-meaning as they were, they were doing him no favours.

And even as I write this, I feel honour bound to tell you, dear reader, that even after Jeff turned his attentions on me I failed to go to the police about it, for much the same reason. It was only after months of harassment (and being urged to sort the matter out by someone far more sensible than me) that I changed my number and handed the texts over to the police.

Sometimes it's not easy to practise what you preach.

Robert Chaplin has not, as of yet, published his book on the Blaneys. Robert tells me that Gerry is continuing to keep things interesting around Garshaigh, wheeling and dealing and generally getting up to all kinds of mischief. Gerry is also a regular visitor to Dora and the children, and seems to have developed a fondness for them all. In some ways, I suppose, that is a happy ending.

Midden Development's plans to build a shopping complex on the Blaney land never materialized. The legal machinations dragged on for several years, but finally the company threw their collective hands in the air, and were never heard from in the area again. At the time of writing, someone has begun grazing cattle on those wild fields again. I'd give a penny to a pound those cattle belong to Gerry.

As can be gleaned from reading this book, I arrived in Garshaigh resolutely determined never to return to child protection work. I was full of doubts about my motivations, asking myself questions about the impact I had had on those who'd had me meddling in their lives, and sick of the pain I seemed to see everywhere I looked.

If you asked me twelve months ago whether or not I had stood by my decision, I probably would have proudly decreed that I had, but the truth is more complicated. I *have* continued to work with children, just in different ways. My teaching eventually morphed from childcare to specializing in sociology and psychology and finally onto child protection, and my journalism moved in the same direction – within two years I was the go-to person for several major newspapers if they wanted someone to write about a child protection issue.

But it was more than that. The Blaney case showed me that while I may not go looking for children who need help, they seem to find me. At any given time I will probably have at least one case on the go that I am involved with on a consultancy basis. This involvement is at many different levels: I have been asked to get involved with national and international committees on policy development, but I also assist in custody cases and help out with child protection issues in schools and crèches. I have worked on one or two cases that attracted worldwide attention in the press – some ended well, others did not, as is the nature of the work.

Do I still find myself upset by what I encounter? Every single day. And I am glad of it. When you come across a child who is hurting, and you don't feel outraged by it, that is when you truly do need to do something else. I am in the lucky position that I can at least try to do something to help.

Finally, and perhaps most importantly, this is a book about grief. Lonnie Whitmore was my friend. I have tried, over three books now, to paint a picture of what our relationship was like: we fought constantly, we competed daily and we could be unremittingly hard on one another. Yet he also knew me better than almost anyone, and could see through my bluster and bravado to the person I am beneath. He was often proud of my accomplishments when I could not even see that I had achieved anything at all. He met every day with a smile and a sense of optimism, and felt empathy for everyone he met, even those who treated him badly. It is only now, many years after he is gone, that I realize just how deeply his death affected me and how long it took me to come to terms with my loss.

This book is my goodbye to him.

He brought out what was best in me, and challenged me to strive to go beyond it. He asked for little in return, and met all of life's obstacles with a smile.

This one is for you, Lonnie.